Did the Smart Apes
Stay in the - -

Phil Trapp

outskirts
press

A major hint that five out of four people
have difficulty with simple fractions.

Prologue

When in crisis, everybody should have somebody to turn to, confide in, trust. My special somebody was Grandfather, a man with no Achilles in his heels, no clay in his feet — a vanishing breed.

He lived in a log cabin overlooking 40 acres of pristine forest, friendly wildlife, and wildflowers galore. An all-season stream meandered through his woods where his ducks and geese could be found splashing about in fun and frolic.

The Currier-and-Ives setting was the inspiration for his theory of brain function which could explain, on the one hand, such brilliances as splitting the atom, unraveling the DNA code, and landing a spacecraft on the moon; and, on the other hand, explain such stupidities as Noah's boarding of flies and mosquitoes, Custer's Last Stand, and the vote for Prohibition.

Science has dealt three crushing blows to our vanity: the discovery by Copernicus that we're not the hub of the universe; the discovery by Darwin that we're not divinely descended; and the discovery by Freud that we're not even the master of our own ship. I think Grandfather should be added to the list for knocking us off our high horse of intelligence, our last legitimate claim to snobbery.

After all, he said straight-faced, since the brain is 80% water, most of our ideas are bound to be all wet.

Narcissism, he claimed, is the main villain. It exaggerates one's intelligence which has one losing the sense of humor and seeing life from its tragic side. The worst offenders, he mused, can be found among our sacred cows, those in our most prestigious professions — lawyers, physicians, scientists, theologians, educators.

He once told me that God was a comedian and we, the audience, were too stupid to realize we were the butt of his jokes.

The day when I graduated from college, a weird thing happened to me. Instead of basking in the joy of having completed my undergraduate degree and now being free to get a job, join the army, or go on to graduate school without parental permission, I found myself down with the blahs. The scene of classmates high-fiving in triumph, parents beaming in reducing their payroll by one, and the commencement speaker touting us as the hope of the future brought no relief. Clearly, a visit with my chief counselor was in order.

In roasting our sacred cows, Grandfather tickled my funny bone which got me to see the comic side of life. It took five sessions to fully rid me of the blahs. Luckily, I thought to tape them.

I share the transcripts of these tapes, hoping that others will enjoy Grandfather's wit in challenging the sacrosanct, since humor and laughter are the key to combating narcissism. In the first session, in presenting his provocative theory of brain functioning, Grandfather pans the biologists and psychologists.

The session was recorded at high noon in the shade of a tall, white oak under a cloudless blue sky.

Tape I

C-90

NORMAL
POSITION (TYPE I)

Grandfather, it's freaky! The college degree, passport to freedom, should have lifted me to Cloud 9. ... I never made liftoff!

> The rites of passage carry no guarantees.

Sometimes I think I'm losing my marbles. The wheels keep spinning but nothing stays in the grooves.

> Not uncommon in academia.

What could be tilting my lamp?

> A clogged C. C., I fear.

C.C.?

> Corpus callosum.

A clogged corpus callosum? Never heard of it. What would cause that?

> In your case, I'd say overexposure to the classroom.

Uh-oh! You're putting me on.

> Why, Grandson, do you suppose the C. C. is in the core of the ol'

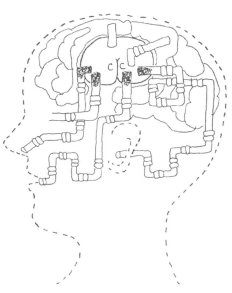

A Clogged Corpus Callosum

apple? To inform each half of what the other's doing? That incidental is common courtesy. Its primary function is excretion, processing waste to keep the brain from perishing in its own muck. (Sigh) Its capacity, were it general knowledge, would stun the thinking world. But if the muck piles up too fast, the pipes will clog.

The brain has an ass?

You've not seen graffiti? Snake oil? A dog-and-pony show? But, stiffen the upper lip. If the pipes aren't jam packed, they'll flush out in due course.

Jam packed? How clogged can a callosum get?

(Sigh) I'm reminded of John Bunyan the Third, better known as Bubblehead.

Bubblehead?

The lad was weaned on bubble gum. It's become his main defense against the outside world. He could never get through an exam without splattering his face full of the sticky globules. But, on the flip side is a bang-up collection of baseball cards. He's got every diamond whiz from the Big Train to the Yankee Clipper, from the Goose to the Moose, from Pee-Wee to Stan the Man.

But, nervous in the service, eh?

This John Bunyan will never make it to the Hall of Fame with his Pilgrim's Progress! Never caught on to academia. Yet, one of those to smile in adversity, he could touch the tender spots, getting a second, and often a third, crack at wiping the slate clean.

Super neat of his teachers.

A grievous disservice. Nothing clogs the pipes faster than test rot. His C.C., reaching the end of its tether, came to a grinding halt and then drifted off into suspended animation.

What's happened to him?

Reduced to a life of humiliations. Like his run-ins with the State Patrol. The sight of a brass badge on a blue background starts his jaws chomping. By the time he's toeing the line for the sobriety test, he's spewing bubbles every which way.

Does he rally?

Impossible! Concentration's shot, coordination's gone. Gravity takes over. He sinks in billows of bubbles and rises in a din of catcalls to receive the C.N.A.

C.N.A.?

Carrie Nation Award. Women's Christian Temperance Union's booby prize for the most DWIs. A plastic bust of the famous hatchet woman, destroyer of the swinging-door saloon, with "We shall overcome" lighting up its base. ... Bubblehead, too, entered politics.

Acin' in! When the mouth and feet are out of sync, cut the losses. Run for office and save the blowing for the stump. What a bummer! Well,

Close to a Fatal Case

5

Grandfather, I'm not a case of the stumbles yet, but sure could use help to flush out the C.C.

(Sigh) He who invents a brain laxative will make a small fortune.

The way I see it, the world's a snake pit, full of wackos and weirdos. Makes me wonder if we descended from the apes or just sprouted out sideways. Do you think we have been given a snow job on this primacy bit? Guess what I'm asking, Grandfather, on the bottom line, are we really that much different from the other animals?

Examine the facts, Grandson. Run over a jaywalker and you're booked for manslaughter. Suppose it had been a stray tabby? Put a cranky old coot out of his misery and you're up for homicide. Suppose it had been a broken-down old nag? Dog bites man and gets quarantined. Suppose man bites dog? … Chalk it up: Homo Saps is unique.

What makes us so?

Brain composition. We humans have two kinds of brain cells — Dum-Dums and Smart-Smarts. The rest of wildlife have brains composed of only So-Sos. Thus, from the cradle to the coffin, we're a bona fide freak of nature.

Far out! Where have the biologists been?

Looking at slides instead of folks. Why, who's ever seen a cross section of humanity on a slide! Retracted in their shells, the turtleheads not only miss the obvious but get bent out of shape with **microphilia**.

Microphilia?

An innocent but, nevertheless, a pathological love affair with microscopes.

You've got to be kidding!

No other way to call it. They fondle them all day and dream about them at night. Even keep a photo of one in their wallet.

To think that one can get so attached to a mere hunk of metal and glass.

The photo carries an inscription: In case of emergency rush imme- diately. The lads live in

Dreams About Them at Night

the terror of going down the tube without their instrument.

Must be the stress of overwork.

The Lord never intended upright man to spend his life stoop- ing and squinting. Divine retribution manifests itself in cur- vature of the spine and loss of peripheral vision.

A terrible price for such a petty perversion.

The old-fashioned family physicians, bedside theatrics their stock-in-trade, rising on occasion to touching performances, blamed it on the sins of their fathers.

A natural development.

One wrote a spine-tingler, *Mystery Gene Strikes Again*. Recounted in graphic detail the wild and wooly escapades of a beady-eyed hunchbacked Peeping Tom who, due to a depraved gene, could only see life from its dark side.

Off the wall! The only clear image I have of my prof is Monday-morning pinkeye. But, we're off the subject, Grandfather. What got you started on your two-cell theory?

The phylogenetic scale. The longer I studied it, the plainer it became that nothing on it approached the stupidity or, on rare occasions, the brilliance of Homo Saps.

Acin' in! Our dumb behaviors are caused by the Dum-Dum cells and our smart behaviors by the Smart-Smarts.

Your grasp of the obvious still intact, Grandson.

But what about all the behaviors that fall in-between — not too smart, not too dumb?

Cellular fustigation.

Run that through again.

Biological warfare. Not a dull moment inside the brain. The cells are incorrigible enemies. Even their odors clash! Quarters are not sought out or granted in the knock-down, drag-out brawls. On a one-on-one, the S-S would win in a cakewalk. Even when bushwhacked, it often shows its savvy and escapes. But more often than not they succumb under the sheer weight of enemy numbers. When captured, they're thrown into slave labor. It's the yoked S-S's before the cracking whip that elevates D-D behavior to mediocrity.

Never A Dull Moment

The interaction effect. A theory on human conflict more unconscious than Freud's! Grandfather, you should publish it.

> And be dragged in irons before the holy fathers of science! Would make the Spanish Inquisition look like a church social!

Scientists close-minded! Resistant to change! Loose and uncaring with the truth! No! I've always thought that veritas was the holiest of their holies.

> Lord love a cuttlefish! The lads revere the truth like everybody else. They worship it as long as they can hang their prejudices on it. Scarce as truth is, m'lad, supply will always exceed demand.

Who'd raise the most flak?

> Wouldn't see the space chaps flipping cartwheels on their launchpads.

What would be their gripe?

> If the facts on us earthlings ever reached outer space, you'd see the biggest powwow ever assembled in the sky, and then see the biggest net ever strung hooked to our poles.

Would sure put the kibosh on space travel, all right.

> Nor would the lads in Congress hoist toasts to my longevity. They know the jig's up once their constituents get wise to the fact that government functions best on smoke and mirrors.

Suppression of truth in a free and open society. So un-American! It seems to me, Grandfather, if it's our noble intent to leave the world a better place than we found it, we'll have to convert hordes of D-D's into S-S's. Can we do it?

Can we rewire skunks into spraying rose water?

Whoops! What can we do?

Fiddle with the essence. Piddle with reproduction.

Genetic engineering?

Abiding, of course, by the laws of **cellular dynamics**.

Another gap in my education.

The first law, pertaining to quantity, states that we have a fixed number of brain cells – 3 to the power of 33 minus 33 to the power of 3 to be exact. When a cell dies - lifetime 3 months, 3 weeks, 3 days and 3 hours to be exact - a new one replaces it.

The brain's gotta be in perpetual motion.

Just one of its many imperfections. The second law, pertaining to quality, states that there are no restrictions to the ratio between the cells.

Meaning?

In theory we could be all S-S's.

How come we're not even close?

(Sigh) The pineal gland runs the show.

Doesn't sound good.

Dubbed the third eye in medical parlance, the pineal dilates when the quality of thought is good and contracts when it is bad. It contracts, for example, on news of national defense or foreign policy which revs up the gears turning out the D-D's.

11

Acin' in! Stupidity cranks out D-D's. What a vicious circle! The Dum-Dums cause the dumb behavior in the first place.

FOREIGN POLICY

NATIONAL DEFENSE

Only a naive observer would think that folks smarten up with age. Those giving that impression are only more clever in covering their tracks. A few justly famous exceptions are Leonardo, Einstein … Babe Ruth.

By the way, the numbers you rattled off on the cells don't exactly jibe with the figures given in our texts. Where'd you get yours, Grandfather?

The Reproductive Mechanism

Guess I've let another one slip out from under the rose. Well, as long as it stays between us and the fence post.

Scout's honor.

Was many moons ago. The heavens dazzled in stardust, and the tiny voices of the woods dazzled in harmony, the best of omens. Then the cicadas changed pitch, nature's subtle way to warn of impending violence. The worst of all omens. The stars vanished, the voices silenced. Then the ripsnorter struck: winds howling, lightening flashing, thunderheads crashing.

You musta been near the eye.

Water battered the shakes, rattled windows, squirted up between floor planks. I snuggled up in a blanket, dozed off, had a dream in vivid color. I was aboard an ark on a great body of water. The sky suddenly turned deep black and the sea vivid red. A typhoon roared in hurling groundswells over the deck. The ark pitched and rolled, nearly capsized. I held on for dear life. Then, the sea stilled and split down the middle.

Eerie.

Out of the parted sea rose white-winged sprites waving a banner containing various combinations of 'threes'. The numbers, in neon lights, burst into flames, jetted, and branded on my brain. The sprites vanished. The sea became one again. I awoke feverish, clammy, bathed in cold sweat.

A red sea … divided waters … angels … burning lights. Holy Moses, Grandfather, it was a vision!

The combination of only threes mystified me until it dawned on me that the three had clairvoyant powers in the mystical world of gods, ghosts, and goblins. In a Road-to-Damascus experience, the code deciphered itself in a blinding epiphany.

The awesome three, the number of the Holy Trinity. Only a full-fledged infidel would deny it a message from the Pearly Gates. … But, on with your theory, Grandfather. What's keeping the S-S's from organizing and zapping the dumbos?

Too few of them. Their only recourse is guerrilla warfare, a tactic good for thinning ranks but not for changing tides. As the world sails blithely along on its course of madness, one looks in vain for the crosswind to change its tack.

Looks like we're facing one of those Gordian knots. Who's got the sword to cut it? Of course, plain as the nose on the face - old man evolution.

Come again?

Rescued by the survival of the fittest. With S-S's superior to D-D's, more of them should keep appearing in the genetic pool.

Darwin's brilliance was dimmed by his far-reaching optimism. The last observable link in the chain of progress was the common fruit fly. Evolution works by fits and starts. Man had more than his share of fits, but his starts have dried up faster than tadpoles on sunny asphalt.

You can't mean it.

The circus whiz, Barnum, observed that a sucker is born every minute. The same words were found scratched on the wall of a Cro-Magnon cave. I rest my case.

The human race hasn't progressed since cavemen?

A measure that stubbornly resists change in our capricious, topsy-turvy world, m'lad, is the coefficient of brain density. The ratio of brain mass to brain volume uniquely stands out as the only constant in the human equation.

Grandfather, I'm getting the feeling you pooh-pooh the theory that we're distant cousins of the chimps.

One must have bitten Sir Charles on a safari to have him treat so disrespectfully that noble beast. Also, it deeply puzzles me that a person with such superior powers of observation had somehow overlooked the jackass.

Gotta admit I see more jackass than chimp in people.

Might also throw the lizard into the hopper. Ever tried checking folks out against the chameleon?

All of this reminds me of the hang-up we have with animals. People poor as church mice have them eating them out of house and home.

D-D's go cow-eyed over So-So's. Has us worshiping them, aping them, showcasing them, stuffing them, even naming bushes and moppets after them.

How did it all start?

Zoolatry has ancient roots. Voodoo priests once slithered about in white robes mumbling the snake chants of the Gorgons. Now the voodoos slither about in white frocks mumbling the rat chants of the psychees.

Uh-oh! Psychologists are today's voodoos?

No discipline, m'lad, is above sorcery to camouflage its ignorance. But those pick-happy lads are shining examples of what hard work and dedication can do.

Pick-happy?

What Hard Work and Dedication Can Do

The pick makes 'em tick, but they do all the picking on themselves. They've been self-mutilating ever since they escaped from the testicles - er - tentacles of philosophy, the octopus of the academic sea. The soul was the first to be picked on. That poor, defenseless thing was picked, plucked, and pitched overboard. Its failure to resurface raised second opinions on its immortality.

Brothers without soul!

Then, the lost souls lost their mind. Little was made of it because only the most discerning could tell the difference. But when they started losing their senses, folks sat up and began to take notice.

Mutilation on all levels! Can it be explained?

When one's at sea, m'lad, a ticked-off octopus can spawn a whale of a castration complex.

I think it's been explained.

The final straw was their flipping out for those thin-tailed albinos.

Albinos?

White rats. The chaps got smitten with rodent fever.

Rat fever! How could that be?

An occupational hazard. The illusion burns brightly that these skittish quadrupeds will bow to law and order. So the lads record every scratch, dash, and squeal. Then the inevitable happens. The random dashings and dartings hypnotize them. They have to be dragged kicking and screaming from their ratpens.

At least somebody's behavior is predictable.

An overstimulated occipital lobe is a shoo-in for the **dipsy doodle.**

Dipsy doodle?

Perception flip-flopping with hallucination. When the chaps look into a mirror, all they see staring back is a cuddly, pink-eyed albino.

Acin' in. If you can't lick 'em, join 'em.

But the fever does mellow them. Eyes soften, acne clears, migraines disappear. Visitors also report fewer tantrums provided, of course, the food pellets closely follow the reinforcement schedule.

Food pellets! Reinforcement schedule! Grandfather, come on!

Grandson, have you never wondered why loony bins have cellars?

The thought never crossed my mind.

To house cages for the advanced cases. The lads prefer little light when they're that far gone.

What do they do down there?

An Advanced Case

17

Press bars ... hoard pellets ... toss darts at cat-boards.

Now that I think about it, our psych prof would often fall back on rat studies to explain human behavior. This has got to be one of the worst who-am-I crises to ever roll down the pike. What can be done about it?

The bull must be taken by the horns. More of the rat has to be brought out of the human and more of the human out of the rat.

How's that pulled off?

With malice aforethought. Every time the chap presses the food bar, the pellet appears shaped like a human. When his upchucking gets under control, a confederate, trained to smile at squints and barings of teeth, stands briefly at the door. He shortens the distance a hair's breadth each day. When finally at arm's length, he gingerly extends a hand.

Touch and go, eh?

Meanwhile a twinkle-eyed albino is electronically wired. The circuit closes on the presence of a human which springs an overhead trap that trips a vial of polecat fluid on a high-speed fan.

No limit to shock therapy.

These skunks, mind you, are no ordinary run-of-the-woods variety. A mutational marvel, they are the quickest loading, fastest shooting, deadliest guns in the underbrush. One shot stuns everything in sight. Rumor has it that the Defense Department is willing to swap two bombers, four jet fighters, and Fort McHenry for one pregnant female.

Bringing more of the rat out of the human

Bringing more of the human out of the rat

Merging Rat and Human

When, Grandfather, is the crisis over?

The fan gets unplugged when the lad behaves more rakish than rattish.

Rodent fever might be worse than leprosy.

Every dark cloud has a silver lining - it does keep one out of the Armed Forces.

We have a knack of getting sidetracked. It's beginning to look like the story in Genesis is gaining ground.

I should hope not.

Why not?

The good book makes no bones about it. God created man in his own likeness.

Strikes me as a reassuring thought.

Think how that dwindles the Lord. To look like us, he'd have to be up to his divinity in D-D's!

I'm digging you. But where does that leave us? We had to get here somehow. What theory's left?

The most unpopular one. The one that's antithesis to narcissism. But I'm not sure you're up to the jolt.

I'll stiffen the shock absorbers.

Genesis was on the right track but flagging the wrong train. Anyone who has closely examined the human anatomy and is still impressed with its proportions would also be impressed with the proportions of the dodo bird!

Gotta admit there are more graceful sights on the planet. Our Maker must have been three sheets to the wind to have come up with such a horrible design. What's your take on it?

Was too narcissistic. Could only use himself as the model.

No! Not what I'm thinking?

Fear so.

The devil's own brainchild?

Could anyone else look like us?

There's gotta be loopholes.

The more one looks at the loops, the smaller the holes get.

How could it be?

When, Grandson, a 100 percent D-D brain coexists with a 100 percent S-S brain, all bets are off. Anything is possible.

What a bummer! Why would an all-knowing, all-powerful deity give the cad breathing room? I mean what's keeping Him from zapping the scumbum?

You've touched on an issue, m'lad, that swelled the hemorrhoids of our church fathers. Let's face it. The Lord could wipe out the scamp with one fell swoop. So what's stopping him? Compassion? Magnanimity? Indecision? Pacifism? Acts of God dispense with those possibilities. The answer has to lie in a twist of fate unique in the realm of aesthetics.

Which is?

The graph of ugliness. Like the boomerang, it goes forward, reverses itself, then heads back.

Meaning one can be too ugly to be ugly?

Meaning that the ugliest ol' bird ever to spit out flames is too cute and charming for the Lord to shut his damper and let him choke in his own smoke.

Or even clip his wings. Gross to the max! But how come we're stuck with paying the piper?

The one glitch in creation. The Lord had whipped up a storm of shapes, sizes, and colors. Then, with all in clockwork order, he lit the fuse and we had the big bang. Cute old Scratch, bug-eyed at the unfolding masterpiece, begged to insert a token memento. The Lord, preoccupied with more important matters, casually flicked a finger in the direction of a small, green-speckled globe barely on his radar screen.

So the scuzbag carved out a critter in his own likeness and dumped it under an apple tree.

The omniscient Lord foresaw at once how the despicable act would throw the animal kingdom into cultural shock. But if he reneged, he would lose credibility with the angels. So, in a stroke of genius, he sprayed the solidifying

Satan Preparing his Gift for the Universe

excrescence with a few S-S's to soften the impact. Thus, although we may look like the devil, we can thank the Lord we're not his spittin' image.

So we owe our arrival on the world's stage to an all D-D brain. We'd be his carbon copy were it not for a few sprouts of S-S inserted by a deity who had compassion for the rest of the animal kingdom. What evidence is there in support of such an ugly theory?

Why, enough to fill Yankee Stadium! Man's first decision had the stamp of the devil on it: Adam and Eve blowing the lease on the garden.

A pair of turkeys, all right. And, to think, all over one lousy apple.

History is a registry of diabolical acts. Imagine smashing the Parthenon … sacking Rome … burning libraries … jailing Galileo … starving Armenians … gassing Jews … inventing the telephone!

Man's inhumanity to man. But where in our biology is the devil's stamp best seen?

In what it takes to perpetuate the race.

Oh!

Demands a hazardous interplay of the sexes in what amounts to coupling - the devil in the details.

There are dangers, you say?

M'lad, the mayhem alone from ill-timed combustion not only shatters the tranquility of nature but is a leading cause of early senile dementia.

I've been blind to the facts.

Onshee Qualfeather and Offbottom Jones can readily attest to the perils.

Offbottom and Onshee? Are those names for real?

Onshee was named after the mountain stream where her folks first met, shot the rapids, and separated from the floating party.

Must have made some ripple!

Offbottom was named after the general - one of our many unsung heroes - who burst into the White House with burning britches to announce the Capitol in flames and redcoats on the march down Pennsylvania Avenue.

So that's how the Mansion caught fire.

Affectionately dubbed "On" and "Off," the ill-starred love-birds were hopelessly mired in pathological indecision. Couldn't decide whether or not to tie the knot. First, it was on; then, it was off. Then on again. When Off wanted it on, On wanted it off. It was on as often as it was off.

As the plot thickens.

They finally ended their shilly-shallying by eloping. Didn't see hide nor hair of them in a blue moon. Then one day they popped up, looking like two wraiths on leave from a dusty tomb.

What happened to them?

Shades of the hysterectomy, the bottom had dropped out of life! They stared vacuously, babbled incoherently. Each pointed a bony finger at the other for their premature entry into senility.

Vegged out before 30. Amazing! Was there a payoff?

The jury's still out. They dragged forth a nose-dripping little bastard - er - dastard whose only functional act was to shred 10 pages of a first-edition copy of *Paradise Lost*, my most treasured heirloom.

Grandfather, if I may so ask, how might it have been done differently?

It shouldn't take a genius to see the advantages of an incubator that could turn out a totally finished product requiring only a self-starter, an adjustable timer, and a self-charging battery. The clone-

The Dastard in Action

maker would then leisurely mix his favorite libation, recline in his favorite rocker, set the speed dial, flick the switch, and sip to his favorite symphony while gestation runs its brief and painless course.

But the offspring would always look exactly like the parent.

Any reason they should have an advantage?

Where would the clone assemble?

Between the ears where there's space to stretch and enough sawdust to stay comfortable.

Acin' in. No prenatal traumas. ... How'd the clone be released?

Through an ear, picking up speed through the wax to flip for a graceful two-point landing. Much to be said, Grandson, to starting life out on your own two feet. The bundle of joy would also debut with impeccable manners, making ear plugs and nose clips no longer essential items in the home survival kit.

A flash! It'd be curtains for the obstetricians. What a buck saver! And think of all the snack bars that could be made out of maternity wards.

Other benefits: an end to paternity suits, child custody wars, crimes of passion.

No more pills, abortions, vasectomies. Even the Pope could become a liberal.

Don't overlook the blessings in dropping the gender. With that clumsy case removed, no telling what grace and elegance might come to the language.

The fact that being bad is more fun than being good is more proof there is more

Ideal Entry into the World

26

devil than angel in us. So what do we do next? Head for the barn, saddle up, and ride off into the sunset?

> The moment has come, m'lad, to share my favorite dream. Have it often and always in color. Recurring dreams in vivid color draw the rapt attention of dream analysts. The dream opens up in a green valley. A lone S-S in a leprechaun suit is stirring a green concoction in a green vat. A puckish grin covers his face. The rustic charm is suddenly shattered by the roll of drums and the clank of boots as over the hill and into the valley swaggers an army of goose-stepping D-D's. They spot green vapors rising from the green vat. They halt, sniff, and swill. Then all is still. The drums stop rolling, the boots stop clanking. The D-D's, to a cell, turn cabbage green and crumble to the turf not to budge for 20 years. Ponder on that one, Grandson. A generation of 'homo' free of 'saps'. ... Holy jumpin' catfish!

A Rip-Van-Winkle knockout punch. A great way to end the tape! Your theory, Grandfather, in combating narcissism, gets one thinking outside the box. In causing us to see what truly lightweights we really are, it has made me aware of how fast our footprints will fade in the sands of time and hence the folly of taking life too seriously. Poking fun at those who are our sacred cows restored my sense of humor which got me looking at the comic side of life. But then on the other hand, don't you think that is a real stretch of the imagination to substitute Homo Saps for Homo Sapiens in the classification system?

> Not if you have a balance of smart cells, Grandson.

Introduction: Tape II

The worst thing that can happen to the intellect, Grandfather pontificated, is to dissipate it in the service of the passions. Thus whenever a topic promised more heat than light, he would suddenly turn hard of hearing. On this occasion, however, the empathic counselor deviated from principle and responded to such hot issues as to where the Lord picked up his mail and what started the boom in church real estate. He even dared the bolts of Zeus in demonstrating how sacred liturgy with a little editing could become a potent weapon against the rising scourge of hypertension – the silent killer of our times.

Grandfather laid out his psychological antecedents of war. It began with the enzyme narcissism which secreted the hormone arrogance which ignited the instinct aggression which fired up the ego to put a chip on the shoulder. If we don't interrupt the chain, he warned, we'll be back to rubbing stones to start the night fires.

In observing that those who beat the drums of war the loudest always manage to keep out of harm's way, he proposed a tactical change. Direct the opening volley at the braid ensconced in the safe rear quarters instead of at the khaki hunkered down in the fighting front trenches.

Grandfather also extended the law of conservation of energy to the psyche. When neural impulses change into consciousness, like when matter changes to liquid, that which is gained never exceeds that which is lost.

In the session, among other things, Grandfather roasted the military and theology.

The taping was done on the bank of his gurgling stream. The orange sunball was slowly bowing out in the west.

Tape II

C-90   NORMAL POSITION (TYPE I)

Grandfather, religion's been on my mind of late.

The Saints keep marching in?

The problem's in the logistics. Nothing adds up. I keep scoring a fat zip. Sure would like to scratch the boards.

(Sigh) Fire away!

I'm what you could call a standard product of the traditional Christian upbringing. God is omniscient, omnipotent, omnipresent. On the bottom line, man proposes and god disposes.

There are those who say man disposes and God reposes.

We call the Lord the Prince of Peace; yet the earth's drenched with blood spilled in his name.

Some love peace so much they'll fight for it! D-D's march to the beat of drums be it for God, flag, or motherhood. But they beat loudest for the Lord. The blood spilled in holy wars would fill the blood banks many times over.

Are all wars caused by the dumb cells?

Only the stupid ones. But, have we had any others?

30

DD's and Drums

I had a history teacher who lectured that man has waged both smart and dumb wars. ... He could catch your attention. I remember his waking up the class one day with this burst of oratory:

> *In the vast stockpiling of human carnage rationalized under noblesse oblige, brilliant commanders have snatched victory out of the jaws of defeat, just as less brilliant ones have snatched defeat out of the jaws of victory.*

(Sigh) Be wary of historians, Grandson. **Egolepsy** can play havoc with the ganglia.

Egolepsy?

An inflammation of the pleasure center. When milk osmotically seeps into the center, it curdles and forms pus. As we know, pus in an air-tight chamber never dries up.

Milk can infect the brain? How'd you find that out?

From a grant supported by Distillers Who Care, philanthropic entrepreneurs who are bonded together to eradicate all liquids prejudicial to longevity. The study, banned in the dairy states, exposed the lethal life-shortening properties of the insidious lactoproteins. Should you ever, m'lad, find yourself succumbing to the lure of milk, be sure to cut it with at least three parts scotch. The pus causes the pleasure center to bloat which causes it to bump the id which causes it to raise its hackles which causes them to brush against the ego, which causes it to go into fits of hee-haws.

Some chain reaction!

Devastating to oversized, oversensitive egos. The seizures, coming without warning, resemble the spasms of nitrous oxide. … Explains why historians are not in social demand.

Nothing unhinges the hinges like laughing gas.

The barrel-chested lads rattle the chandeliers, making St. Vitus' dance look like a pokey two step.

Gotta be embarrassing.

Demands a fast cover-up. The few that are still in circulation have a barrel of side-splitters to wipe the egg off the face. An optimist is a historian showing up at a funeral.

Their conventions must be slapstick.

A tickle-tortured ego is no laughing matter. It can tip the balance between the real and unreal.

Like a schizy coming-out party?

More on the order of fantasy upstaging reality.

If that's not lamp tilting, what would you call it?

Organized schizophrenia. Facts do get twisted and bent out of shape, but never go into free fall. In some quarters it is called revisionism.

Smacks of deception. Shouldn't something be done about it?

Only if you take the lads seriously. For my part, I'd hate to see their horizons shrunk. Would be as diminishing as a Santa without beard and potbelly.

Just how, Grandfather, does organized schizophrenia work?

Gordon Strangefellow is a classic case. Called Flash because he's spaced-out much of the time. Found his natural niche in history. But the lad was born with the brain circuitry of a sleazy sleuth.

Spells trouble for sure.

Santa Diminished

He was invited to address a highfalutin underground society, the Stock Sons of Boston. To be a double S.O.B., one's line has to go back to the original colony of Plymouth. Imbued with the fire-and-brimstone of Jonathan Edwards, the famous pulpit-pounder of the old Bay colony, the boys date our moral decline to the demise of such time-honored practices as woodshed whippings, public floggings, thumb removals, and crack-of-dawn necktie parties.

Why do they stay in the underground?

For fear of reprisal from Quakers, Unitarians, League of Women Voters, American Civil Liberties Union, groups threatening Mafia diplomacy to settle fundamental doctrinal differences. Tongues began wagging on learning the title of Flash's speech: "Captain John Smith: America's First Traitor."

Smith of Virginia a turncoat! Now that's sleuthing at its sleaziest.

Flash had smelled out a cabal with Smith, Pocahontas, and Rolfe the ringleaders.

John Rolfe, the tobacco grower, whose curing process opened up foreign markets?

That was the tip-off -- the sudden expansion of the tobacco crop. The Indians weren't dying like flies from consumption, as the wily spy had reported, but were conking out from carcinoma of the lungs. Rolfe's part of the conspiracy was to smuggle the deadly plant to the United Kingdom - with the intent, of course, of wiping her out.

How that would've changed the course of history! What happened?

The Czar had grossly underestimated the crusty ol' Cockney who not only survived but thrived on the carcinogenic weed.

I missed a cog. How'd Russia get into the act?

Finding a rare document is a shot of adrenalin to an organized schiz. Revives him like a blood transfusion to an anemic. Flash discovered a long-lost letter from the Czar's daughter. The nubile princess wrote glowingly of the courts of Europe but ignored Buckingham's. Flash deduced she'd been scratched from the tea list, a snub which could only mean a cold war was in the mill between the bulldog and wolfhound.

A conspiracy theory.

> The clincher was the visit of the fair Pocahontas to London's royalty. She arrived in the pink but overnight turned ashen white and then bluish gray. The Scotland Yarders had come through once again with colors flying - er - flying colors.

With the size of those potatoes, you'd think the Yard would be shouting the scoop from the rooftops.

> Was evident to Flash that the Corps was addicted to the weed and would perish in cold turkey were it outlawed. Not willing to put their fate into the hands of the fickle hoi polloi, they took the blood oath of silence. Anticipating international fame for his brilliant breakthrough into the origin of east-west tensions, Flash had to be heavily sedated when the reviews came out. ... Furthermore, the double S.O.B.'s never invited him back.

The perils of milk. But surely, Grandfather, there must be some historians with normal pleasure centers.

> Not if they're worth their salt! Marcus LaChoice made a bundle devising a paper-and-pencil test that measured only egolepsy. Although just 25 items, the test totally separated the plums from the prunes.

Doesn't seem possible.

> Shaken more than one pillar of academe. Their dash to the ocean would have the lemmings eating their dust if the whole truth ever tumbled out. Only five items are for real. The rest are fillers.

You're putting me on! Five test items can plumb a discipline as devious as history?

> Would I ever purposefully lead you astray, Grandson? The ramifications of a bloated pleasure center apparently have yet to filter through your cortical convolutions. LaChoice, dumb as a fox, padded his test with 20 items that academicians since Hector was a pup believed to be sine qua non for success but which, in fact, have little to do with it.

Items relating to what?

> Intelligence … verbal fluency … abstract thinking … logical reasoning … higher-order concept formation …

Whoops!

> The e-items alone are the only truly reliable predictors of eminence.

Must be fantastic discriminators. What are they?

> I suppose releasing one won't gum up the works. The item reads: All my life: (a) I've hated clouds; (b) I could take them or leave them; (c) they brighten up my day; (d) a day without a cloud brings a night with the runs. … All egoleptics check (d).

Clouds, a security blanket. No wonder historians can't agree among themselves — they woolgather in cloudland. But, then, couldn't you say the same about actors? artists? musicians? poets?

> LaChoice had grandiose plans. Results from his private survey revealed that the heaviest milk guzzlers were in the creative arts. If he could tag their future luminaries, he would be able to buy the Washington Monument.

Washington Monument? Why would he want that?

(Sigh) Tis a tale to tug the heartstrings. Began with innocent-looking tinker toys. The moment young Marcus opened his first can his fate was sealed. His passion to collect them was overpowering. They soon filled his room, the attic, the basement, the garage, the fruit cellar ...

What did he do with all of them?

Built obelisks: ... small ones ... medium ones ... big ones ... jumbo big ones.

A true wacko.

Then one day his martinet mother caught him in compromising behavior. In a fire that lit up the sky, she pitched in every tinker toy. The message was uncompromising - there would be no more obelisks.

Grounds for child abuse.

Served only to fan the flames of passion denied. Marcus became a prisoner of our national Capital, pining the hours away with eyes transfixed on the biggest obelisk of all - the Washington Monument. Finally dawning on him the meaning of his obsession, he knew there'd be

Marcus at his Best

no joy, no peace, no freedom of mind until he could claim it for his very own.

But surely such an historic monument would never be put on the market.

During a great depression even the Executive Branch can get practical.

The price tag must have been a pretty penny even back then. Guess poor Marcus couldn't swing it.

His monumental dream was shattered! Everybody aced the test. No discrimination whatsoever. Marcus sank into a deep, irreversible depression.

No! You mean to say that everybody in the fine arts has a pleasure center out of plumb?

Milksops all! The man whose genius led to these startling revelations is now a permanent resident of a back ward. He gleefully passes the hours mindlessly building innocent obelisks out of risque tinker toys. Sparks occasionally flicker in his eyes to betray the once raging fires. As the good book says, the Lord giveth and the Lord taketh away.

I think we've wandered from wars. Just how would a smart war be fought?

By having the smart cells manning the phones at the command post.

What would be the strategy?

Aim high. First shot would signal open season on the generals. They're the thread, bare as it may be, that keeps the khaki from unraveling. But, with their itchy feet, they could be anywhere from the Kashmir to the Klondike. The mop-up could take as long as six weeks.

Nothing like the sight of falling stars.

In the fervor of wars defending the honor of the Lord, Taps would also have to sound for the colonels. With the generals gone, they'd be sitting ducks for the snipers as they idle away time shooting craps in the rear tents, the flaps open for ventilation.

Can see it wouldn't take deadeye dicks. What about the majors? Would they, too, have to become national heroes?

Once the command passes into their hands, the white flag would soon be flying. The boys are too enamored of the officers' club to take war seriously.

A novel strategy. How did you come upon it?

Serendipity. As a longstanding buff of cryptanalysis, I was at the time breaking the Hokumwatti Code.

Hokum what?

A code of a remote mountain tribe based on arcane hieroglyphics. It took me over a year to crack.

That's stick-to-itiveness, I'd say.

But well worth the investment. It gave me access to the only account of the most extraordinary battle ever waged. It transpired in the hinterlands of the Himalayas where these two warring tribes had been hammering and tonging at each other for over 200 years.

What sacrifice for country!

The youth of both tribes, up to their epaulets in patriotism, fought inspired. Heroes were anointed daily. Reenlistments flourished. Promotions accumulated. By the time of this historic encounter, there was a general behind each fighting man.

Half of the armed forces generals! Gotta be a first.

There was another first. Because the press had hyped-up the skirmish to an Armageddon, the generals reassessed the situation. Anticipating a passel of reporters and photographers, the two high commands rushed their uniforms to the local, quick-service laundry.

Some blast! Holding final troop inspection in skivvies.

Since there was only one facility, all uniforms ended up, naturally, in the same laundry. That night a mysterious explosion took place. The laundry was blown to smithereens! Not a stitch or star anywhere in sight.

Was the battle called off?

Honor demanded holding to the agreed-upon schedule. The braid borrowed khaki for the big shootout.

The generals fought the battle looking like soldiers!

An unparalleled scene in the panorama of human warfare. With the opening charge, the puffing, slow-moving brass, unaccustomed to no respect or preferential treatment, began dropping like gnats in the path of DDT.

Must have been a slaughter.

Shortest battle ever recorded. Not a general was standing when the whistle blew for coffee-break. The boys relaxed and shared bread and booze. When somebody happened to ask what the war was all about and nobody remembered, they shook hands, went home, and raised goats, the main source of income in the Himalayas.

A flash! Smart wars are not only short but picky for whom they play Taps.

A far cry from the wars where the fat cats stay home to make millions and the young Adonises stay in the fields to make cannon fodder.

Fat cats?

Warmongers, m'lad. Fathers rebelling against sons - the sequel to Oedipus Rex in which Laius, the wronged father, gets revenge on Oedipus, the wronging son.

What madness! What can be done about it?

I sent a brief note to the commander-in-chief proposing he demote the generals at the top of the pay scale to reduce the national debt.

That had to send tremors through the Pentagon.

Merely a stopgap measure as lads with a spit-and-shine mentality would soon be back wearing the star. The real purpose was in the P.S. suggesting he bugle the rest of the braid up at dawn to do five chin-ups to evaluate their fitness for war, trusting the few who survived will rush into early retirement.

How did the President react?

Swiftly. He dispatched the FBI to my woods and cancelled all leaves for his firing squad. Suspecting I was part of an international conspiracy, he also sent a crack unit of the CIA to the front.

Didn't know we had presidents who could act so decisively.

Was a godsend that he chose those units of his command. Unable to work together, they were more of a nuisance than a threat. The entire siege turned out to be a struggle of one-upmanship.

Acing in. Everybody out to impress the home office.

Their bungling tactics took a toll. Whenever there was a lull in the action, I'd swing from a vine and yell "banzai" in Swahili. This would trigger a barrage of gunfire and a rapid setting of booby traps.

They never winged you?

Did all their basic training on the open range, never learning the trick of ricocheting bullets. The silly accidents kept mounting. Whenever I stumbled upon a victim of a caroming slug or a tripped trap, I bagged the remains and sent it C.O.D. to the White House. This not only controlled the buzzard population but cut the red tape for next of kin.

Thoughtful.

Gave a deep sigh of relief that the President decided against reinforcements. Was having nightmares of seeing myself smeared on the tabloids as the coldblooded Hun who had methodically wiped out the cream of the crop - in the full bloom of life.

Would have been a tragedy surpassing the Alamo.

The President finally recalled his tattered remnants and turned my files over to the National Guard. The militia, unable to pin me to uprisings on the campuses, riots in the ghettos, revolts in the prisons, or marches on the capital, quietly closed the case.

Custer came along a generation too soon.

Was relieved to hear that the units have since recruited to full strength. They are, after all, indispensable to our national defense.

How does that follow?

When our enemies see the film highlights of the boys in action, they're bound to get the opinion that our national defense is in desperate straits and is in dire need of an overhaul, giving us the all-important psychological element of surprise.

Grandfather, the nagging question I have about wars is...do you think we'll ever see an end to them?

Not as long as the narcs keep active.

Narcs as in narcotics?

Narcs as in narcissism. Although too small to see and too light to weigh, they pack the wallop of TNT. And, like TNT, a sudden surge in heat can detonate them; the heat, however, coming from the aroused emotions.

They must carry some charge.

Enough to blow pussycats into tigers, puppy dogs into pit bulls. When the narcs stir, the adrenaline flows. Only when

43

folks feel less big and important will they be more inclined to sit and talk than to stand and slug. Narcissism, Grandson, has killed more folks than napalm.

Pride goeth before destruction or whatever. So it's the narcs that keep us rattling sabers and beating drums. Which brings us back to religion. Grandfather, what makes their drums beat so loud?

Freud blamed it on mass neurosis; Marx on bourgeois opium. Truth is, neurotics do jump to drums, and drummers on dope do double the beat. In tandem they can rocket D-D's into space. (Sigh) Dum-Dums orbiting in space can change religion from a tonic to a toxic.

Can see the D-D's of the Lord's fanatics soaring highest. But, once up there, what keeps them going?

Pompous pietism. Ever try slowing down a chap who can only sweat holy water!

Lord spare us! Salvation, then, hinges on spotting them before lift-off. Any clues?

They pray for the last ride to be in a horse-drawn caisson and to bow out to the roar of Winchesters. (Sigh) And they also do the wretched unthinkable. They garnish the martini, the ultimate cocktail, with an onion!

The Philistines! But, why the rifles at the lowering?

When the mortal coil's been shucked, m'lad, there are souls who need all the boosting powder they can get.

Grandfather, how do you suppose opium got into religion anyhow?

Goes back to the halcyon days of Roman decadence. Living at the time was a struggling young architect and part-time fisherman by the name of Pete. One dreary morning with the drawing boards bare and the fish ignoring the bait, he was approached by the Hades connection.

What for?

To design a house of worship. Old Scratch, depressed because of the chronic heat, suspected that the sight of mortals writhing before diatribes of hellfire would bring him high relief. Pete had all the necessary qualifications. He regularly desecrated martinis and daily lit candles for a hero's exit. The quid pro quo was the guarantee of a fresh supply of onions and the promise of a rifle squad to salute his departing soul. Pete touched off a design race.

Design race?

When deep into their cups, architects let slip their secret pact with Mephistopheles. They exuberantly raise and click their glasses in toasts to onionized martinis, to horse-drawn caissons, and to smoking Winchesters.

This somehow reminds me that Mom continues to offer up litanies for your Sunday morning activities, or rather, lack of them.

Though the odds are continually reduced on your Mother getting eulogized as a repository of gems, bear in mind, Grandson, that she does have a heart of gold.

Uh-oh!

Houses of worship pack the greatest number of folks into the least amount of space, optimal conditions for the maximum exchange of carbon dioxide. Air once removed revives Dum-Dums.

What will be your defense on the Day of Reckoning when your attendance record comes up for review?

Covered that base when I was a shaver in knee breeches.

What happened?

The day was hot but not as hot as the rhubarb we lads got into over an ambiguity in the Lord's resumé - his local address. Several noses got rearranged when it became evident that a consensus was not in the cards.

Must have been a blood bath. What was your stance?

Had none. Hadn't the foggiest idea where the deity collected his mail. Pondered that night if I'd ever know. Then the scientific solution popped out of the blue.

Science meddling in metaphysics?

Wasn't easy. Had to sacrifice my Sunday morning comforts for Judeo-Christian austerity. (Sigh) There's enough church real estate these days, m'lad, to shelter the down-and-outers the world over!

The architects did go on a spree. But what was the study?

That was simple enough. Merely had to make the rounds of all the houses, squeeze into a back pew with pad and pencil, and count the grayheads.

Why them?

They were the blood and guts of the experiment.

Think I'm lost.

Elementary, Grandson. Pews were meant for praying and who prays harder than he with kith and kin down! We all know that the Great Healer would rush to the aid of the afflicted, provided, of course, he could hear the distress calls. Naturally, to be able to hear them, he'd have to be within hearing distance.

Naturally.

Thus, the house that overflowed with grayheads, those lucky sinners whom the good Lord heard, healed, and let sin to a ripe old age, could claim local headquarters.

Had to be your red-letter day, but a black-wreath day for nose straighteners. Which house, Grandfather, creaked the loudest from the joints of old sinners?

Where but in a world full of devils and curmudgeons could the patience of a Job be rewarded with the luck of a Jonah! Nobody had a monopoly on anything – apart from high-buckled shoes and osprey-plumed hats.

The agony of science - the negative results. What did you make of it?

The Lord, in his infinite wisdom, goes fishing on his day off.

And you followed suit - not looking too worse for wear! Grandfather, while on the subject, where do you think the big mailbox is, anyway?

Over a cocktail one day, I paused to ponder the ultimate. What would it be like to be all S-S's? What would be my cake and ale? Then a fly, his radar gone amok, nosedived into my drink. My thoughts abruptly sifted to the D-D's and what would be their druthers. All kinds of flotsam and jetsam poured into my stream of consciousness - honky-tonks, clip joints, gun shops, brothels, flea markets ... family reunions. To counter the rising dyspepsia, I conjured up images that would have the D-D's passing gas.

Like wine, cheese, and a good book?

On target, lad. Dum-Dums go colic whenever the rumblings of the guts make harmony with the rhythms of the soul. To shorten a long story, when the debris finally flushed out, the insight floated in: Set the inner dial to the higher frequencies and listen for the signals.

Got it! To get the sigs, synchro the vibes. Did the beeps come through?

Mirabile dictu! There were the tinkling of tiny bells at the leafing of a tree, the blooming of a flower, the leaping of a deer.

God's in the great outdoors.

The bells also tinkled at the sonnets of the Bard, the "Bel Canto" of Caruso, the *Duchess of Goya*.

God's getting perplexed. A grande dame sharing top billing with Bambi?

The deity is where beauty is, Grandson. When the Lord mastered the trick of being in two places at once, he had conquered time and space. He could be anywhere at any time. But he's running out of space. The wing-weary birds and bees are losing ground in their efforts to cover up the encroachments of the ugly.

My heart's starting to bleed for the men of the cloth. Seeking inspiration, they do their searching in Houses of Worship.

> The more intense a search, the more tunneled the vision.

Doesn't seem right.

> The croup and rickets are drawn to mortar like flies to wood outhouses.

Disease is no respecter of persons.

> The setting would give the Fiend himself high relief from the cares of the day.

No! Houses of worship sanctuaries for devils?

> In tending to the moral life, m'lad, I've given little thought to tracking down the spoor of fallen angels. However, should there be a scholar so enamored of the perverse as to relish such an undertaking, chances are he would rank the meetinghouses high on his starting list.

Do you suppose those of the calling might have second thoughts on the Lord's favorite spot in his Creation?

> The blackcoats show a trace of insight.

Where?

> In the larynx. Notice how they rant and rave from the pulpit but speak ever so softly to a rose. The cords know when the Lord's within whispering distance.

A flash! Meetinghouses should have escape hatches so if the hell-fire-tirades get too hot, one can exit without creating a commotion. Wonder why I haven't thought of this sooner?

An old survival ploy of D-D's is to dangle carrots and get folks off and running. Who stops to think on wild goose chases!

Us meets the enemy and them is us or whatever. ... Grandfather, if the Lord's not hip on masonry, what should we do with all the Houses?

As the devil's advocate, if I were czar of the universe or sultan of the solar system or mere caliph of planet earth, I'd post an edict to stack the roofs with gargoyles.

Those ugly things.

What better fits the stripes of the scamp?

Uh-oh! Houses of worship shrines for Satan?

Saints forbid! While I'm not into marching to Gabriel's horn, neither am I into goose-stepping to the devil's organ grinder.

Think I'm getting confused.

Put it in the perspective of history. Every age has its curse, its plague, its black cloud. The albatross on our back is a rising diastolic. Today, an ounce of prevention is worth a pound of diuretics.

What's shooting up the pressure?

Venom in the soul. It heats the blood. When it reaches the boiling point, hoses begin to pop. The coolant with the least side effects is catharsis.

Acing in. Catharsis at the church. Open the valves, let out steam, and live through another stroke-free day.

Bull's eye, m'lad. However, a little tinkering would need to be done with the liturgy to get the best results.

Like what?

Like substituting the prosecution of the scamp for the sacrifice of the lamb.

A mock trial?

The courtroom melodrama is why old judges never die. A trial could be tailored for each type of poison: one for the bluenose, the redneck, the bleeding heart, the bloodthirsty. Each house could plug its own antidote.

Grandfather, did you just see lightning?

Zeus, I must warn you, is a charter member of the old guard. He doesn't cotton to upstarts or meddlers. Shall we quit while we're still ahead?

We live but once. Damn the bolts. On with a scenario.

If the gallows be our lot, let the punishment fit the crime. Let the heresy begin by tampering with the Roman liturgy, granddaddy of the Christian creeds. Let us detox the bloodthirsty, souls but a heartbeat away from apoplexy. The trial could follow the format of the mass.

People are more comfortable with the familiar.

To set the tone, we'd have the gargoyles belch black smoke and the organist bang bars of Faust as the frenzied crowd, scenting blood, make beelines for the best seats. The trial begins with the Gloria, tidings that the grand jury has indicted old Clubfoot. Cue signs for cheers go up. The choir bellows out a chorus of "Hallelujah". Silence settles in for the Credo, list of charges, atrocities committed on humanity under the guise of the Lord's will. The collection-plate brigade shout "kill, kill" in a rising staccato chant. Hearts start to race, bosoms heave, feet shuffle as the groundswell picks up momentum. Witnesses offer testimony at the Offertory.

Who might they be'?

Those with the highest concentration of venom per centimeter of soul: a bigot, a pompous ass, a goody two-shoes. They pour out their lurid tales. The cry for blood gets louder. Incensed nuns break out bean shooters. The sergeant at arms, a crusty old mother superior, pounds her gavel in a losing cause.

If there's a mercy seat, may it be full of mercy.

The gospel, the closing argument, is an eloquent summation of the human travail that leaves not a dry eye in the house. The jury, twelve dimple-cheeked altar boys, receive instructions at the Consecration. While they huddle in deliberation, wine is freely imbibed to fortify the sclerotic arteries for the Benediction, the verdict of the jury, the signal for cathartic release. When the roar of guilty booms out, pandemonium breaks loose. Flash cards for primal screams and rebel yells flutter in the chancel. Bells clang; balloons rise; confetti descends. The trial closes with the choir belting out verses of "Onward Christian Soldiers" as the color guard of the Knights of Columbus, in asbestos armor, march the fire-spouting demon to his execution. ... Te deum! Mankind is avenged.

You forgot the communion.

A grievous oversight. Nothing lowers the diastolic of the bloodthirsty faster than a cannibalistic feast. Dragon pâté on croutons is to be served with the wine.

Sure glad Mom's not here. ... What would be the role of the clergy?

The holy fathers, resplendent in saffron-dyed vestments, would wear the birettas of chief prosecutor and high judge.

I suppose the church paintings and sculptures would have to be boxed. Can hardly see them fitting the decor of a trial.

The motif of the new art would be the time-honored scales of justice - an eye for an eye and a tooth for a tooth. The murals would show Old Scratch in tar and feathers ... drawn and quartered ... burning at the stake ... boiling in oil ... dangling by his horns ...

Got the message. Our asses are too tight in the snake pit. They've got to loosen up. Seems to me that the men of the cloth should be offering a helping hand. ... So, why aren't they?

Guess they'd rather preach than massage.

Makes one want to think.

Miracles can happen!

Do you suppose the philosopher Descartes in making his famous declaration --"I think, therefore I am" -- knew how high he was setting the bar?

Hippocrates, father of modern witchcraft, making his declaration -- "I fart, therefore I am" -- wins the cigar.

What a bummer! The guts make the decisions and the brain tries to make them look good. Can we ever really know what's true from what we want to be true?

It's only human to fill the missing pieces to the puzzle of life with wishful thinking. It eases the anxiety of the unknown. But data should never backpedal to dogma. While it's wrenching to drop old beliefs, when the evidence mounts steadily against them, clinging to them can ultimately be even more wrenching.

Tape's about shot. Grandfather, the kaleidoscope's been flip-flopping but as the pieces begin to fall into place, I think I see a light at the end of the tunnel.

Make sure, laddie, that it's not the cannonball express.

Introduction: Tape III

An enviable statistic on Grandfather was his health record up and through his octogenarian years. His mind kept its edge, his step its bounce, and his eyes their hawk-like acuity. He could spot a bee in clover before the rest of us could spot the clover. Yet he ignored the common rules of longevity. He loathed exercises. Strolls in the woods to talk to his plants and animals were his compromise. He impressed on me that the quality of life was much more important than its longevity.

This was not to imply that Grandfather treated lightly the subject of health. Far from it. He shed light on why our country that ranks tops in medical schools, clinics, and research centers would have so many of her people in poor health.

In this session, he panned particularly the medics, morticians, and Departments of Agriculture. An example of his droll wit was his lampooning of physicians whose grasp of reality, he stated, is very tenuous. They all advise their female patients not to have babies after 40. Apparently, they must think the female is capable of having more than 40 babies.

He softened my frustration over the blahs in saying that if all folks put their problems out on a clothesline, they would likely bring their own back in.

The taping was done in his beloved woods. The wildflowers were out and wind was soft in the pines.

Grandfather, what baffles me most is the state of our nation's health. The ads are full of body builders and health perks. We have advanced technology and high standards of sanitation. Spa and recreation centers make big bucks. Joggers cram the countryside. Yet, one can walk into a physician's waiting room at any time of day and find standing room only.

It's the naked truth. We make the best soap but put the puniest bodies in the suds.

Why would this be in a land of milk and honey?

Too many folks backing the bugs.

No! Who could be so perverted?

Med schools, hospitals, Department of Agriculture - to name but a few.

Uh-oh! Grandfather, I sense that you're about to desecrate more sacred cows.

Never was into worshiping bovines. Milk is pernicious to health whatever the udder, but it's beyond the 'pail' from sacred cows. The odor of sanctimony turns it sour.

What went sour in our med schools?

They began turning out practitioners.

What's the harm in that?

A matter of values. Deep in their aortas spurts the lifeblood of the **psychopomp**.

Psychopomp?

In the days of antiquity when Athens was a great commercial center, many common trades graded themselves up to a profession. Corpse collectors, for one, hung out the shingle psychopomp and doubled the price.

Physicians envious of morticians! Why would you ever think that?

Observe the way they gaze at passing hearses, get dewy-eyed over formaldehyde, perk up as pallbearers, cut a mean rug at wakes, always the last to leave at gravesites – all the dead giveaway signs of a frustrated psychopomp.

So that's why the docs duck out of sight when a patient croaks. Scared of blowing their cover. Now that's really spooky.

M'lad, the world's chock full of folks who'd mortgage the family farm to be custodian of the corpse. Most give up the dream, lower their sights, and settle on a related occupation.

What sort of folks?

Football coaches, truck drivers, stockbrokers, comedians, college administrators …

Stockbrokers?

More cardiac arrests occur in one day in the market than in a month in intensive care.

Comedians?

Who invented the deadpan? The sick joke? And what kills faster than slapstick!

I can't believe college administrators.

Among the worst. A day never passes without sending a memo to an underling: "Publish or perish."

No relief in sight.

Notice how actors peak in the death scene, how musicians pump up their heels in the requiem, how clerics ratchet up the rhetoric in the eulogy, how the military wear out the hyperbole in bestowing medals posthumously.

Mind-blowing! Whatever got you started on this line of thinking, Grandfather?

Newspaper polls. They all ranked the obituary column tops in popularity, running rings around the comics and advice-to-the-lovelorn. Had me taking a closer look at the fabric of heartland America. The warp and woof of it is that folks are cut from two cloths: those warped on death, 99 percent, and those "woofed" on life, one percent.

Far out!

(Sigh) The bird watchers society ranks a distant second to the C.W.S.

C.W.S.?

Casket Watchers Society. The ghouls meet on Memorial Day at a closed-down boneyard in the boondocks. After a pig-out on beer and hot dogs, Taps is sounded and banshees flutter out from behind ivy-covered tombstones to wail in the climactic event of the day: coronation of the king watcher of the year.

You're pulling my leg!

The furor last year was over Jeremiah "Crossbones" Stretcher - er - Fletcher. He set a Guinness record of 1224 watches. ... Several of the old-timers fainted.

That's more than three lowerings a day.

The rules clearly state that watchers need not know the deceased. With competition stiff and stiffs on the rise, no stones are left unturned to rack up the numbers.

Crossbones Fletcher

Like what?

Hot lines to parlors, confederates in emergency rooms, candy to the florists, booze to the clergy. With their hot rods fine-tuned, polished, and gassed-up, the boys are ready to rev at the first sign of a wreath.

To a jazzed-up rendition of "Nearer My God to Thee," a solid lead casket covered in a black velvet shroud is unveiled. Some claim it's made in Japan; others insist the Bronx. All agree it costs a small fortune to ship home to the trophy room. I'd say it's worth every shekel since they make the perfect storage bin for old home movies and family albums

This brings to mind a psych prof who chilled the class one day describing a kinky perversion, necrophilia, the gist being that the dead are preferred to the living.

Had a brief encounter with one of those parlor pests. The hardest part, he confessed. was adjusting to the cold shoulder. What attracted him most was impunity from charges of alienation of affection.

No!

If you want my private opinion, I'd say the chaps have gone overboard for a passive partner.

The thought's coming through, Grandfather, that you're treating lightly the subject of death.

Always considered death, Grandson, a 'grave 'matter.

Meaning you've dug deeply into it?

Could write 'tombs' on how to kill a dead horse.

It does make sense that people who get their jollies over cadavers would be green-eyed of the undertaker. Who logs in more time with the dead?

61

Clear thinking.

But my lamp's tilting. Books talk about necrophobia, fear of the last heartbeat. But you say death's a popular show.

Only when the other guy's the star attraction. 'Heartening' to know you're ahead on some counts! As to its popularity, have you ever been to a funeral with empty seats?

I think we've digressed. Back to the MD's. If they're such frustrated psychopomps, why didn't they enter that field in the first place?

Raised that question to several members of the hippocratic club. After hemming and hawing, they confessed to chickening out on the entrance test.

Why'd they do that?

Our mortuary academies, committed to keeping numbers low and burial costs high, send each applicant a blown-up photo of a thinned-out graduating class walking on water, with a footnote that the list of drownings is available on request.

So, the applicant takes one look, gets drunk, and applies to the nearest med school.

The sick, after all, are the next best thing to the dead.

I think I've grossly underrated the undertaker.

Never sell short the coffin retailer, m'lad. Disingenuous to the core, that picture of death warmed over, that ferryman who ferries one over the River Styx, has a heartbeat on rush days that compares to the winners of the daily double.

Rush days?

The holidays. The days when D-D's go on a rampage: blood stains the highways, the Klan breaks out the sheets, scorned lovers counterattack, parents of teenagers OD. ... The days when gravediggers break shovels, blister thumbs, and double their pay in overtime.

The fun days do seem to have their stats.

Peak season, of course, is the Yuletide. The one humane act of the Puritans was to outlaw the holiday as a pagan feast. It cut the death rate in half. I once spent a nativity eve at our local palace of rigor mortis taking measurements on the staff. Their jovial, back-slapping greeting flabbergasted me until I learned they had just bumped up the price of coffins another 100 percent. The lads were in fear of a revolt. Folks at times, you know, can be 'revolting'.

What did you find?

Pandemonium. Brain temps in the red. Brain waves off the chart. Retinas straining on their moorings. Long lines at the water closet. All in all, a scene of whirling dervishes doing the danse macabre.

Praise the Lord and pass the urn. May there be peace in cremation. ... Back again to the MD's. How do they deal with their frustration?

With sublimation, the noblest of the defense mechanisms. Energy is selflessly directed toward perfecting the symbiotic relationship between host and parasite. It takes consummate skill, m'lad, to maximize the interaction without permanently losing the host.

I would guess.

Ozzie Overhill is a case in point. Looks like an old bantam rooster who had fought his way through a barbed wire fence. Ozzie's under the care of a top specialist who's kept him looking this way for fifty years.

But, Grandfather, physicians do cure people.

Nobody's perfect, Grandson. Medication errors, communication goofs, staff shortages, hard-of-hearing patients can botch the best-laid plans.

Mindboggling to think that the caring family physician would be in cahoots with the bugs. What tipped you off?

Chartophilia. The symptoms always surface in the presence of a disease-free specimen.

Chartophilia?

A malfunctioning of the pupillary reflex. The eyeballs expand, protrude, and lock on a chart.

A frozen, bug-eyed stare?

Often the nurse has to resort to the martial arts to get eye blinking resumed. Patients, only recognized by charts, get passed on the streets like ships in the night.

So the docs aren't cold fish after all. What got the disorder started?

The tail wagging the dog. The pill peddlers began treating the disease instead of the patient. But, to

Chartophilia

64

give the devil his due, it does make the practice of medicine less repulsive. Charts don't smell, are less painful to the eye, and never talk back.

A tough combination to beat.

Can have its awkward moments. I'm reminded of Pinky, a prankster with a rose-tinted bulb for a schnozzle. Miffed at the long delay in the outer cage, he switched charts with a skid-row boozehound. The chart gazer, poring over the wrong peaks and valleys, advised him to end his martini lunches if he had any hopes of lasting out the month.

What was Pinky's next move?

Rolling his eyes in disbelief, Pinky calmly asked to see his medical transcripts. Doc went livid. Pinky kept up the harassment until the Doc got so hopping mad that he pledged to deliver personally a case of gin each month that the pesky ingrate beat the odds.

What happened?

Pinky became the beneficiary of a regular supply of high-quality imports. The Doc, convinced that he was privy to a rare medical phenomenon, withdrew into seclusion to prepare a major medical address: "Hepatic plasticity: Never sell short the lasting power of the liver." ... Reaction was swift.

I would guess.

His portrait graced the entrance hall of every liquor emporium in the land. ... The original 42nd-Street booze brigade voted him an honorary member. ... The great state of Kentucky gave him a lifetime key to their finest distillery. By the same token, the Woman's Christian Temperance League served him forged extradition papers, the A.A. hanged him in effigy, and the Vatican volunteered its best team of exorcists.

Must have taken the nation by storm. How did the bubble burst?

Pinky, not wishing to appear overly greedy, replaced the chart after 120 hand-delivered cases. The doc admitted his blunder at the next medical conclave and got a standing ovation, a mea culpa so rare in the medical fraternity.

Grandfather, this has the markings of a contrived experiment. Did you, by chance, play a part in it?

Grandson, questions like that set in motion the Fifth Amendment.

Still boggles the mind to think that the white coats would be in cahoots with the bugs.

The sweet innocence of youth! I also would suppose you are totally oblivious of the skullduggery that routinely goes on in the Chamber of Horrors.

Chamber of Horrors?

The outer cage. Generally referred to as the waiting room.

I'm totally oblivious.

Nothing, m'lad, in the annals of sinister plots, holds a candle to it.

Uh-oh!

Begins with a receptionist looking like an angel and smiling like a saint as she schedules appointments to assemble the

most atrocious of the man-hating mini-bugs. When the misanthropes arrive, she sprays the menagerie with an aphrodisiac disguised as a room sweetener. Eroticized bugs, m'lad, have the table manners of starving barracudas.

MISS ANGEL

PLEASE SIGN IN   WALK INS WELCOME

Misanthropes in the Waiting Room

DeSade must have had daughters.

Patients are detained two hours on the pretense of a backlog of emergencies. My one excursion into microbiology confirmed that it takes precisely two hours for sexually aroused microorganisms to make a landing, establish a beachhead, and launch a synchronized attack.

But, Grandfather, there are patients who leave the chamber without complications.

The price for that obnoxious behavior is incarceration in the bug factory.

Which brings us to Public Enemy Number Two. What crimes have the hospitals committed against humanity?

(Sigh) Would take the quill of a Dante to do it full justice. Those gloomy edifices happen to be the Shangrila of the microbe kingdom. Nature's plagues, which are her retaliation against our crass assaults, are mere pablum compared to what comes out of their high-tech incubators.

Why is this so?

Basic economics: out of bugs, out of business.

But, what about the antiseptics and antibiotics? How can they be good for business?

Clever decoys to divert attention from the main front where elite troops mass for a five-prong blitz against the inner man. The execution runs like clockwork. The first prong, delay and torment, gets underway at admissions.

Shades of the chamber?

The value of a crowded vestibule is not overlooked. The torment is legend: fine-print insurance exclusions, signed legal papers to protect the incompetents, non grata room extras, urine demands on returns from the water closet. Such frontal assaults on the human spirit weaken the will to live.

What's the second prong?

A steady inflow of uninvited guests. One is no sooner bedded down in rags mortifying to a scarecrow when the shylocks file in to extract their pound of flesh. The bloodlettings drive the stake deeper into the body's vitals.

I've wondered why a vein's never hit on first try. What happens next?

The honoring of an old medical maxim: "When in doubt, cut it out." Diagnostic testing drags on until the green light flashes for the scalpel. The hard-and-fast rule of the operating table is to cut long and sew slow.

Why so?

To get bugs into the greatest number of working parts.

I believe we're at the fourth prong.

It attacks the last natural defense against misery - sleep. Every soul, Grandson, rich or poor, pure or tainted, famous or faceless, is entitled to a peaceful night of rest.

Right on!

Not so with our Florence Nightingales. Armed with oversized anal thermometers, they make their lethal lunge when sleep is deepest. Should Morpheus, the god of dreams, induce somnolence after that brouhaha, they strike again with blinding lights to dispense sleeping pills.

Come to think of it, Frankenstein was the brainstorm of a woman.

Rooms are assigned with meticulous care. Nothing dicey about it. One snorer to a double room and loud hackers to flank the thin-walled singles.

Conspiracy at every turn.

The coup de grace is a waxing machine with a defective muffler that roars down the corridors at night. The night shift is top-heavy in black belts. Hell hath no fury like an old geezer deprived of shuteye.

The last prong, Grandfather, whatever it might be.

It heeds the old saw: Strike while the iron is hot.

Meaning?

Stuff what remains of the remains with D-D chow.

Why that?

It was the D-D's who let in the varmints in the first place. The treatment plans make no bones about it. Stay with a winner. Keep the D-D's at maximum strength.

How does a patient ever get discharged?

The saving grace is the savings account. It's closely monitored, and the moment it hits bottom, a special staffing is called. Everyone is suddenly of the one mind that all's been done that can be done. The cadaver is released stone-broke but with tales to spellbind the clan when the jug gets uncorked on holiday gatherings.

Yet in spite of the conspiracies, Grandfather, you've somehow managed to escape them. Don't know of a soul who can match your health record. How do you do it?

Persnickety over victuals, Grandson. Have always given the matter top priority.

Drawn any conclusions?

D-D's thrive on such indelicate hybrids as sprouts and broccoli. Crops so utterly insensitive that even cussin' won't stunt their growth.

Never did like spinach mixed with my oysters.

Then we have the succulent tomato. The slightest raise of voice causes its leaves to droop. A most discerning plant, it doesn't suffer fools gladly.

I've noticed they fill your garden.

Attend to odors. Plants are like wines: the more exquisite the bouquet, the more subtle the fragrance.

You don't season with onions and garlic?

> Does anyone! S-S's savor the mild scent of the distilled grain, the faint aroma of the immersed olive.

I'm taking notes.

> Don't ignore hues. Cells also differ sharply on that dimension. S-S's dig the reds like apples and cherries and, of course, tomatoes. D-D's dig the greens like broccoli and turnip greens. The color of stewed broccoli reminds me of the color of stewed sailors.

But, then, there's the green olive.

> The exception to the rule, provided it's not mutilated. Clip its tail, excise its core, stuff its innards, and the noble fruit has lost all integrity.

The formula then is to choose food on the basis of looks, smell, sensitivity, and character.

> We are what we eat, less what's eating us.

What about the meats? What can top a juicy steak? A rare roast beef? A plain ol' hamburger?

> What can better incarnate the death wish!

Uh-oh! I think you've just hit the main nerve of the cattlemen. They happen to be the toughest hombres in the West.

> They've already contacted the bounty hunters. Happened after my keynote address to the C.C.B. - "Castrated Christian Bulls" or was it "Christians for Castrated Bulls?" Well, for sure, they were all bullish on castration.

Who exactly are they?

> They're the last vestige of the Old West, they have pledged to consume a T-bone a day, to wear the genuine – not the drugstore imitation – cowboy boots and ten-gallon hat, and to buy the leather-bound novels of Zane Grey. The decal on their pickup trucks reads "Steer a-Head," and when reciting the Lord's Prayer, they substitute steak for bread.

Wow! Bet not a hundred Christians are in the club.

> On the night I addressed them, they boasted a million dues-paying members. The sterile bull, m'lad, has become canonized under the stars and stripes. Come to think of it, I've yet to receive my honorarium.

Not enough bull in your speech?

> I used the occasion to sound out my theory on A.A. It was poorly received, beyond their ken. They drowned me out with a barrage of moo-calls.

A.A.? Alcoholic Anonymous?

> A.A., Ass Actualization. A phenomenon, I regret to say, that's been sadly neglected in scholarly circles despite its sharp rise in evolution. Perceptive students of gross anatomy recognize the high relationship between ass flexibility and quality of life.

The full impact didn't hit me till puberty arrived.

> The birds and fishes, creatures with the flexible glutei that can raise their ass above the head, have captured the envy of the S-S's. Compare their worldview to that of the cows and hogs, idols of the D-D's, whose glutei can barely lift their hindquarters above the ground of their everyday trudgings. Ah, laddie,

when you get right down to it, what can surpass the elegance of a smooth, high-flying ass!

Why would a fish want to lift its ass above its head?

How else would it get to the bottom of a lake?

A.A. should be in print. Must be a publisher somewhere willing to take the risk. What about a university press?

Those flibbertigibbets are so sensitive to the south end of a north moving horse that they break out in hives on seeing the word even in the good book.

Maybe you could blunt the edge by using "derriere".

A rose is a rose is a rose; and, by any other name, it will still be a rose; but a high-flying derriere will never make lift-off.

'Tis a bit heavy, all right. ... Well, Grandfather, while we still have a little tape left, what's your main beef against the Department of Agriculture?

Don't wish to mislead you. Some folks swear by the USDA. Teeth extractors and eyeball adjustors continue to sweeten their kitty with cash in unmarked paper sacks.

Why incognito?

A habit they acquired after I sent them the results of a minor study I'd done.

What was that?

An isolated piece of statistical trivia. When the USDA was or-ganized, only one chap in a thousand wore specs or plates. On its centennial celebration, the figures had reversed: only one chap in a thousand was not into prostheses. ... Dentists and optometrists open their conventions with a minute of silent prayer to the USDA.

Why are those stats so little known?

After getting the report, the executive boards called a joint session and voted unanimously to underwrite the medical expenses for the lifetime of my dependents in exchange for the data. Occasions do arise, Grandson, when one must rise above principles. In a curious coincidence, after the deal was consummated, the material vanished in a barn fire.

Stunning stats. How do you account for them?

Mother Nature's revenge. She's making her intentions all too clear. She is slowly but methodically wiping out our sense organs. Before long, we'll be a species sans sight, sound, smell, taste, and touch.

Mother Nature's Revenge

Even losing our touch?

> When the old lady gets her dander up, there's no stopping her. And no folks ruffle her feathers more than those meddling Agri chaps.

What have they done to her?

> Take the plight of fruits, one of her favorites. They're in an identity crisis. It's hard to tell cherries from plums, plums from peaches, peaches from melons. I'm not even sure when I'm eating blueberries these days.

The old-fashioned apple pie is gone forever.

> Their tinkerings with nature have led to tough-skinned hybrids that defy heat, cold, drought, and disease.

Sorta takes the fun out of farming.

> Their arsenal of artificial fertilizers, insecticides, herbicides, and repellents have led to silos bursting at the seams. If left to her own devices, Mother Nature would never tolerate such extravagances.

The agricultural revolution seems to have gotten out of hand. But what's the beef about hybrids, Grandfather?

> Their chemicals. They secrete an odorless, colorless, tasteless, invisible poison that slowly atrophies the left hemisphere of the brain, the side that controls thinking, judging, reasoning … and voting.

If the poison's invisible, how'd you discover it?

> While casually strolling on the local campus one day, I noticed a motley crew of Agri's shuffling along with their heads

slightly tilted. I mentioned the abnormality to a passerby who, after squinting, failed to see any slant. Other folks paused, squinted, and saw nothing. A quiver of doubt began to sweep through me. Were my powers of observation that superior or was my contact with reality that labile? I had to find out which!

What'd you do?

I bearded the lion in his den. Made a wager with my old crony, the Cow Dean, that I could spot his boys on sight alone.

Did he take you up?

He gave me his usual inscrutable smile and doubled the bet. He assembled two hundred instructors, half Agri's, and marched them in random order briskly across a stage. Working from a different hypothesis, he had everybody in shirt and tie, shined shoes, and well-sprayed with Lysol. I sat in the front row with a pointer.

Who won the bet?

I pointed out all but one of his boys, many of whom, I might add, later petitioned for compensation, complaining that the brisk cadence had brought on dizzy spells and chest pains. Some even spent the night in the emergency room.

Never know who's out of shape these days. But a fantastic hit score.

Bothered me that I had a miss. On checking it out, I learned that the dean's ulcer had been flaring up over a rumor that his only daughter, a vacuous but sweet dairymaid, was rendezvousing on the sly with one of his licentious, rosy-cheeked instructors. He had higher aspirations for her. He hired a shamus disguised as a new staff member to flush out the whelp before tenure locked him into the ranks of the untouchables. The shamus played his part well. He won the distinguished teaching award that year.

Talent can be that misjudged in academia! ... What did you do next?

Had to find out what caused the heads to tilt. I first pondered the wryneck syndrome, a pathology of the neck muscles. A group of volunteers nixed that hypothesis. The issue had to lie in higher tissue. The local slab artist agreed to weigh the hemispheres of the next 50 Agri's under his jurisdiction. He found that the left one was consistently lighter, the amount depending on the number of age rings on the skull.

Age rings! I thought they only appeared on wood.

The lads for certain were up to their eyebrows in mischief. I grilled over a dozen to ferret out the truth. Tough nuts to crack, they protested their innocence until threatened with truth serum. Rather than risk exposing the high crimes and misdemeanors of their checkered past, they owned up to petty larceny. They'd been snitching grub from the experimental farm.

Where the latest varieties of hybrids grow.

The boys broke the first law of economics: it never pays to get a free lunch.

Did they buy that?

Who ever reasons folks out of beliefs that weren't acquired that way in the first place!

Grandfather, you accused modern agriculture of creating a food surplus. What's the harm in that?

Elementary. More chow leads to more mouths; more mouths to more bugs; more bugs to more health centers.

Guess we'll never face a bug shortage.

Psychopomps have few natural enemies. I have, however, come up with a foolproof scheme to slow down their booming business. It consists of a two-column chart. I list the "dos" for health in one column and the "don'ts" in the other. I keep the chart updated.

Where do you get your info?

I'm on everybody's mailing list: the head society ... the foot society ... the skin and bones society ... the blood and guts society ... every society claiming some part of corpus real estate.

But those are the societies run by the frustrated psychopomps. It doesn't tally.

Only up to a jackpot, m'lad, providing, of course, you put the dos in the don't column and the don'ts in the do.

Slow on the uptake. And what's the title of your chart, Grandfather?

The triumph of the Smart-Smart cells.

Introduction: Tape IV

Grandfather was the first of the clan to enroll in college, and he never lost his lust for learning. A true Renaissance man, books lined the walls of his cabin. One could be taken randomly and notes would be found on the margins. The most dangerous of the illiterates, he asserted, are those who are ignorant of being ignorant.

Although a strong supporter of education, he was critical of the products being turned out. Students are passively taught what to think instead of actively trained how to think. They become proficient in memorizing facts but poor at solving problems, which he considered is the quintessence of the educated person. Reform should start in higher education where theories of education originate.

Therefore, in this session, his roasting of sacred cows in education began with college administrators who he complained are more concerned with the looks of their vita than with the looks of the final product. His panning of the faculty was reflected in his humorous story of the prof who timed his watch in boiling water while holding the egg.

In typical fashion, Grandfather's proposals for getting the academic ship back on course made definite waves. The insight I got was that my blahs, in part, were due to the failures of our education system.

The "awakening" took place in rocking chairs before the dying embers of his wood-burning stove. It was unseasonably cool.

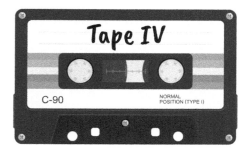

Grandfather, the more I think about it, the more I'm convinced I'm a casualty of our educational system.

Find little to refute that.

I'm not alone. Many are feeling the same way. Reform is in the air.

Long overdue. The academy has become a travesty of the ideals that conceived it.

What went wrong?

The motor. It's working backwards. When it revs up, it heats the Dum-Dums and chills the Smart-Smarts.

That bad, eh?

Look at the fallout. They never stir before noon, read nothing but comics, watch nothing but soaps, hear nothing but hillbilly. To escape boredom, they blast horns, litter roadsides, play pinball machines, and cash in food stamps for cigarettes.

Gotta admit our track record's suspect. Teachers are constantly grumbling that the yokels can't read, write, or spell. Grandfather, if given free rein, what would you do? Revise the curriculum? Raise standards? Fire the teachers?

81

You're missing the boat, Grandson. The first law of reform is: don't piddle at the middle, lop at the top. The opening salvo should be at the top guns in education, those who are heads of our universities. They are responsible for the quality of our education.

Who are they?

They're called, among other things, administrators.

Higher Education—The Fallout

I know very little about them.

They rarely venture into the open, preferring drawn shades to sunlight. A bevy of secretaries guard their privacy, programmed to say "out of town" or "in conference" to would-be intruders. But don't let the low profile bamboozle you; they're the birds who call the shots.

If one were to risk full light, what would he look like?

Haggard, strung-out, potbellied from the banquet circuit. He'd be most likely attired in a Hong-Kong suit, tie-matching socks, and sporty wingtip shoes, a dress code in force even for such idle pastimes as duck hunting and skeet shooting. But his hands are what truly set him apart.

Hands?

They're asymmetrical. One of the flippers, usually the right, is badly deformed, an eyesore mostly hidden in a pocket. This,

82

of course, strains the suit, causing it to wear unevenly and get pitched before its time.

Weird! What brought on the deformity?

A corroding brain stem, the part of the brain that regulates self-control. First sign of cortical malfunctioning is an outbreak of **memomania**.

Memomania?

A compulsion to write memos. An addiction that soon spreads to questionnaires, surveys, accountability forms, and 50-year plans to meet the crises of tomorrow. The overworked fingers swell into lumpy, necrotic-looking protoplasm.

How'd you ever stumble onto this?

I've always agonized, Grandson, over paper waste, an unconscionable way to deplete natural resources. When I saw more and more loggers invade the virgin woods with their long-handled axes and crosscut saws, I decided it was high time to get to the bottom of it.

What'd you dig up?

Memomania

A scatological statistic. More trees end up in memos than in water closets. The ugly head of the memo, m'lad, rises highest in nature's gallery of rakes and rogues.

The brain wasting more paper than the ass? Against natural law! What did you do next?

Took a closer look at the villain. Sneaked up on the local campus and pilfered 10,000 memos from faculty wastebaskets. Began sorting them.

Must have been a humongous task.

Any schoolboy could have done it. They fell into two distinct piles: 50 were short, clear, genuinely informative; the other 9,950 were rambling, opaque, pointless.

What'd you make of it?

There obviously had to be two memo centers in the brain, one run by the S-S's and the other, by the D-D's. Not so obvious would be locating them.

How'd you approach it?

Head on. I sat and wrote a brief, intelligible memo. While writing, I moved the fingertips of my free hand over the scalp. The nerve endings spotted a warm area over the frontal lobe. I had located the smart center.

What sensitive nerve endings!

The advantage of a balding pate is that it can keep one in touch with what's going on in the head.

What about the dumb center?

A horse of a different color. I wrote a long, senseless memo and detected nothing. The center had to be somewhere deep inside the noggin.

Covers a lot of territory.

Had an excellent lead. A study done in vivo, given short shrift because it reported a flurry of synaptic misfirings at the base of the stem, findings contrary to current theory.

That's probing a long way into a live brain.

The scalpel plunges deeply to tap the wellspring of the emotions. The misfirings had to come from a Dum-Dum center.

You just had to prove it.

Dame Fortune smiled on me. Amp Voltmore, a bright, untenured instructor, dropped by for a visit. An eye twitched, fingernails were down to the nubs, and a foot kept tapping the floor.

What was bugging him?

Neurology. Grants had supplied him with the best hardware in the business, but whatever he ground out was already in print.

Competition in science must be brutal.

A breakdown seemed imminent when the dean sent him that short, clear, genuinely informative memo: "Voltmore, reference Policy Number 000001 - Publish or Perish."

Antsy Amp was certainly under the gun.

I told him to stick with the faith. There was a project tailor-made for him. All he had to do was chloroform a dozen or so administrators, place pad and pencil in their hands, inject electronic needles, and throw the switch. If all went well, he'd have tenure in the bag.

Voltmore had to be in high cotton.

His immediate reaction was constrained elation. He mumbled that his lifelong dream was to make a giant contribution to mother science. Then his tic returned. He doubted that the president would jeopardize his top lieutenants for the mere advancement of science.

Amp Voltmore

He had a point. Prexy would sure be on the hot seat if his loyal vassals went up in smoke.

I assured Amp he'd get the full cooperation of his leader if he slipped him the aside that the real purpose of the study was to raise the art of confusion to the level of a science. Mastery of chaos would put him, the president, in the catbird seat. He would now have the skill to spin out memos so obtuse and opaque as to counter effectively whatever plans the young turks had in the mill for pulling off a coup.

Did that ease his fears?

Almost. His symptoms flared up again at the thought of the neurological damage that might result from driving a needle all the way to the stem. The lad was in worse shape than I thought. I had to remind him of the subject pool. The hard part would be over once he pierced the skull.

That should have done it.

Amp sprinted to his lab, feet barely touching ground.

Were there any hitches?

Nary a flaw. Fifty white-knuckled deans and vice-presidents, whistling the alma mater going under, validated the theory.

Voltmore must be world famous. Those are the kind of discoveries that win Nobels. Strange that our science teacher never mentioned him or the study.

It was never published. The president lost his naiveté at a cocktail party and went bonkers. He charged into Voltmore's lab, smashed the equipment, burned the records, and ordered his staff to make crank calls at all hours of the night.

Do nice guys ever win?

It drove Amp out of academia. It preyed on my mind until I bumped into him several months later. He was no longer foot tapping, the tic was gone, and his nails were fully grown out.

What was he doing?

A handball instructor at a racquet club. The pay was better, the hours were shorter, and the work easier. Furthermore, there were no death threats or memos in the wastebasket.

Nice guys can win. ... Back to administrators. What can be done for their corroding brain stems?

(Sigh) Lead poisoning is irreversible.

Lead poisoning! What brought that on?

Job insecurity. The pressing duties and responsibilities have them sitting for hours at their desks, sucking mindlessly on pencils. The leeched-out lead from the graphite compound accumulates alarmingly. Contrary to popular folklore, surplus lead is stored in the stem, not in the butt. When the overflow valve kicks in, corrosion begins and self-control, like paraffin in the midday sun, melts slowly away.

Job Insecurity

Why, Grandfather, would one risk brain damage even to be an administrator?

It's the sticky, age-old problem of burnouts in academia. What to do with them? The classroom is a fishbowl. Retooling is cost prohibitive. Cyanide is unchristian. Outright dismissal, with the numbers involved, would precipitate a recession. The humane solution is to quarter them in a large, fireproof building in a remote section of the campus.

Why the isolation?

As long as universities remain tax-supported institutions, it behooves them to see that visitors get the best possible first impression.

Why a fireproof building?

The jittery lads have never mastered the meaning of fire exits. The alarm bell sends them racing pell-mell to the elevators. When they open, the doors jam in the crunch that follows. Rank is always ignored in a panic.

You also mentioned a large structure.

Incompetence proliferates exponentially. The tasks of a few become the labor of many. Only on administration buildings do you see annexes attached to annexes.

Never have liked annexes. They never blend well with the architecture. ... The picture gets bleaker and bleaker. What can we do to brighten it?

First step is to revise the job titles and descriptions.

Reform begins with the flow chart?

You're on the boat now, Grandson. The more impressive the label, the more chutzpah the D-D's display. Pompous titles like President, Chancellor, Dean, Director simply stir up campus unrest.

What would you suggest?

Down-to-earth tags like custodian … groundskeeper … bodyguard. The savings in pencils alone would more than pay for the clerical help.

Can see that badges with those titles would hardly strike terror in the heart. What would be their new duties?

Cost-efficiency studies recommend that division of labor be based on strengths. Assignments, therefore, should be made on the amount of brain loss. The more recent appointees would be given outside duties. The remainder, the more injury-prone, would work inside under closer supervision. The tags for the outside workers would be Groundskeeper I, II, or III, the rating depending on the hours, pressures, and aesthetics of the job.

Such as?

Those operating the fruit stand, seasonal work, little stress, pleasant duty, would be Groundskeeper I. Those removing dog dung and pigeon drippings, lightwork, regular hours, but painful to the sensibilities, would be Groundskeeper II. Those picking up deadwood, long hours, back-breaking, emotionally exhausting, spiritually draining, would be III's.

What about the inside workers?

They'd be tagged the bodyguards since their primary duties would involve protecting life, limb, and property. Those frisking students at classroom doors for concealed weapons would be Bodyguard I. Those hiding in labs to nab thieves and vandals would be Bodyguard II. Those guarding the purses of the secretaries at coffee breaks would be the III's.

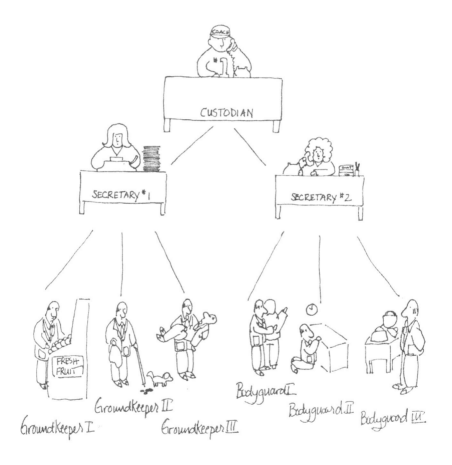

Revised Flow Chart

But III's the top grade.

Never underestimate the value of secretaries, Grandson. They're the hub of the wheel that keeps the blokes - er - spokes from flying off in all directions.

Who'd be the fund raiser?

The custodian. The one on campus most skilled at bilking - er - milking the alumni, the football coach. His important fund-raising activities would get underway the moment the gridiron season is over.

Nobody better at collecting the cabbage.

To keep priorities straight, his success would be measured by the shekels raised rather than by the games won.

Wouldn't that space out the alumni! They'd be climbing walls if it meant supporting academics to keep a winning coach.

The collapse of the flamboyant lifestyle with the wearing of the blue collar, symbol of an honest day's work, would likely cause a breakdown of the nervous system. A generous extension of sick leave should ease the distress of the long convalescence.

A kind thought.

Salaries should also be generously adjusted. Regardless of the amount of brain loss, the highest grade should never be more than a notch below the lowest grade of the secretaries. Such preferential treatment, of course, would end with future appointees who would be spared the trauma of entering the golden years with an inoperative stem.

Seems only fair to reward those with long and loyal service.

Trash receptacles would have to be spaced every fifty feet on the campus as memos will continue to be cranked out. Old habits, like old generals, die slowly.

I'm swinging into your program of reform. Reassigning administrators according to their level of incompetence elevates the faculty into the vacated slots. They become the birds who call the shots.

(Sigh) Impressions notwithstanding, they are the Illuminati.

Uh-oh! What went wrong with the faculty, Grandfather?

Their intellect. It got entangled in the web of **instructophobia**, a terror of the classroom. Students are capable of triggering catatonic seizures. The eggheads, plagued with nightmares of sleeping dragons waking up, approach the halls of learning with the spooked look of knights-errant tilting at possessed windmills. The survival ploys are legend. Some chew garlic to empty the front rows. Some mainline formaldehyde to stiffen the nerves. Some lecture to the blackboard; others stare in the right direction but wear opaque shades. Many lower the blinds, cut the lights, and show flicks - a life-preserving resuscitator called audiovisual aids.

Resuscitator?

Vital signs return to normal when the room is dark and the enemy snoozing.

Fear does such strange things.

These, of course, are the more extreme cases. The majority will stay the course, face the foe head-on, and ward them off with spates of oral diarrhea.

Oral diarrhea?

93

Trivia ad nauseam. An endless efflux of nitpicking facts. Flapdoodle of the sort that clogs the C. C. Right, Grandson?

Right on, Grandfather! But what should be going on in the classroom?

Why, making distinctions that make a difference. Teaching students the skills and techniques of how to think. The halls became hallowed when teachers began polishing diamonds in the rough and honing swords to slay dragons.

Yet, you're willing to make the profs head honchos!

An opium pipe dream were it not that the phobia can be cured.

What would it take?

Brainwashing of the order of Chinese water torture. The skittish egghead is to take a long, deep breath at each dong of the clock - the dong soon grates the nerves like the steady drip of water - and chant: "Students are not dragons. They only look like dragons. Dragons make fire. Students make smoke. What ho! The world is going to be all right." The chant must go on dong after dong after dong.

Seems simple enough.

The most difficult part of therapy since appearances strongly influence beliefs. Those unable to make the leap should be channeled into administration.

Seems right.

But for the great majority, the power of the word ultimately wins out. The eyes suddenly dilate and there comes a cry of magical wonderment: "It's true! It's true! The monsters aren't dragons after all." The euphoric insight sets the stage for the next phase of therapy.

The Cure

Which is?

Convincing the egghead that a lie is the truth. Much easier to make truths out of lies than lies out of truths because D-D's are old hands at dealing with lies. There are, in fact, three lies to convert. The chap is to take a deep breath each morning before his shaving mirror - deep breathing softens shock - and chant: "Students love to learn ... Students love the classroom ... Students love their instructors. What ho! The world is going to be all right." He then downs a slug of whiskey to relax the tightening vocal cords.

Only one!

The day finally dawns that gives rise to that special inner glow called psychotic insight. The poor devil babbles out: "It's true! It's true! They love me. They love the classroom. They love to learn. Holy sweet Madonna!" ... The egghead suddenly loses his skittishness.

The phobia is gone and all is well?

Delusions of grandeur have to crystalize to retain their power. Therefore, it's imperative that the instructor's first genuine eye-to-eye contact with students verifies the psychotic vision. The classroom must be seen as a beehive buzzing with intellectual activity.

Goodbye blackbird! Grandfather, you'll never see more deadbeat drones than those in the classroom seats.

What do you suppose would happen if the instructors were given carte blanche control of tickets to all nonscholastic events - sports, dance marathons, cockroach races, mud wrestling, beer chugaluggings, goldfish swallowings - and meted them out only to the most deserving?

Acin' in! The beehive would suddenly be buzzing with make-believe Einsteins.

In playing charades, the imposters might discover that spiked punch and laced cubes are not the only means to a high. They might end up getting hoisted by their own petard!

The scenario's unfolding. I see happy-go-lucky administrators sailing memos at trash cans, fearless faculty brushing off stings from the hive, and gung-ho pledges burning midnight oil for seats on the fifty-yard line.

The winning razzle-dazzle, to coin a football metaphor, would have the sheepskin taking the snap from the pigskin.

Then, the trickle-down effect. Teachers going into the little red schoolhouse to heat up, not chill down, the Smart-Smarts of the tiny tots.

Believe you're getting the picture, Grandson.

Of course, it all hinges on curing the goosey faculty. After which, I suppose they'd be in charge of registration, fees, graduation, whatever.

> Great balls of fire! Leave the nuts and bolts to the secretaries. Surest way of losing your faculty is to make bookkeepers out of them.

Oh!

> M'lad, you can lose your wealth, lose your health, lose your fame, even your good name. But for god's sake, hang on to your faculties!

Introduction: Tape V

Modern Science, Grandfather lamented, has lost its charm. Grand old theories have been shunted to the dustbin. Minutia has replaced substance. The esoteric has taken over.

No one can accuse Grandfather of this falderal. He lauded macrotheories. In this our final session, I savored his wisdom on such cracker-barrel goodies as: What defines a moral person? What's the key to the good life? What makes marriages go on the blink? What's the one sure sign of mental illness? What sets lawyers apart from the rest of the race? What's the secret to winning a Pulitzer? What changes the most in old age? He dismissed the esoteric as a mere window-dressing of ignorance and thoroughly championed Occam's Razor, the principle of parsimony which states, in a nutshell, when the choices are roughly equal, always take the simplest.

Moderation was his answer for maintaining the balanced life. Too little or too much even of a good thing skews the scales. He chose his favorite cocktail, the martini, as his example. He used the female mammaries as his rule for consumptions – one is not enough, three is too many.

We moved along at a fast clip, leapfrogging from subject to subject to get it all down on a single tape. My mood was upbeat, having finally conquered the blahs.

It was a very special occasion. We were celebrating Grandfather's 89th birthday. We had chosen the site of our first gabfest, his favorite white oak. Only this time it was night and the stars were out in full number. We had a pitcher of martinis, putting moderation on temporary hold, to propel Grandfather elegantly into the last 12 months of his octogenarian years - as I duly recall it.

In the blur of memories following our violating his rule of martini consumption in polishing off the pitcher for the occasion, one stood out ... his telling me if I ever should doubt that the smarter apes stayed in the trees, go to a zoo, go eyeball to eyeball with a chimp, and observe his superior stare.

Tape V

C-90   NORMAL
                                        POSITION (TYPE I)

Grandfather, super news. I've been accepted to a full year of study in Paris, France, which means I'll be spending more time in the academic jungle.

Skoal, lad. But watch out for the jungle rot.

I'm still fussing about my career goals. At the moment, I'm leaning to philosophy.

(Sigh) At least it's not English.

What's the advantage?

English hounds end up driving sight-seeing buses for Greyhound. Philosophers, unable to get the hang of vehicles beyond four wheels, end up in the fields picking peas and beans, a much healthier way to earn one's bread.

So, here's to the pea-pickin', string-bean philosopher! Speaking of picking, since this'll be our last rap for a spell, is the ol' apple up to it?

Why not! With the heavens all lit up, and we a mite lit up ourselves, there's no telling what manner of cat might pop out of the bag.

I'll drink to that! Let's tee off with a heavy. I've always thought of you, Grandfather, as one of my profs would put it, a dust-bowl empiricist. One who sees life without rose-colored glasses. One who calls a spade a spade. Now that the 89th niche has been notched on your tree of life, I'm sure the thought's come to you that there might not be too many more.

Nature has a way of closing all circles.

But I'm laying odds that having lived the full life, you'll cross the bar without so much as mussing a hair.

Stuff and nonsense! Feathers will be flying at the end. To those who love life, death is a donnybrook.

I can see there's a big difference between fighting death and fearing death.

The gut difference between the cells. Smart cells battle the grim reaper down to the final slash, while the dumb ones throw in the towel at the first swing of the scythe.

Do not go gentle into that good night. ... Let's talk some about the moral man. I took a course in ethics, was taught all the ethical theories, but given no answers.

Par for the course.

Even buttonholed the teacher for the rules of the good life and got the run-around that he'd let me know the moment he found them. Grandfather, I bet you're not afraid to take the bit between the teeth, because I know of no one with stronger moral vibes.

Never ceases to amaze me what a little lubrication can do to the perspicacity. I know of your vexation. Who gets a straight answer out of philosophers? Ask them if the sun comes up in the morning and dollars to doughnuts they'll ask which sun.

I guess morality can get rather abstract.

Poppycock! Even a birdbrain can grasp the concept. The moral man acts in the service of his S-S's; the immoral man serves at the pleasure of his D-D's.

Can't be more straightforward than that.

Since meat for one is poison for the other, there is no middle ground.

No compromise?

No back and fill, as skippers of the old cutters would say.

A man of principle, then, sticks to his guns come hell or high water.

That's the quick of the matter. But keep an eye on the slyboot always lipping the virtues. He's covering up, just like the bore who brags on being self-made. Being self-made, granted, beats not being made at all!

Grandfather, let's get down to the basics. What's the payoff for living the good life?

Sweet happiness.

That's it? Sweet happiness?

An angst-free psyche is no small trove.

But I see black hats all over town not exactly casting Jeremiah's shadow.

You're confusing pseudo-happiness with the real McCoy. Many a bumpkin has been taken down the primrose path by the D-D's who have more scams than mutts have fleas.

What are some of the worst?

Palming off kiss-of-death schemes in can't-miss packages … masking poison in sugarcoated pills … gussying up trash in silver-lined boxes … dumping scrawny pigs in fat pokes …

So, when the dingbat wakes up and finds out he's been snookered, his sweet lemons turn to sour grapes. The subtleties of the D-D are finally-working their way through my convolutions.

An old standby is getting the greenhorn to chase a rainbow and hitch his wagon to a star. Lord'a'mercy, lad, have you ever seen a star drag a wagon?

The cruelties of the real world. Yet, Grandfather, it seems to me you've not only dodged the scams of the D-D's but have found the inside track to the pleasures of the S-S's. How'd you do it?

Ah, laddie, you've just touched upon the crowing - er - crowning event of my life.

I did?

After putting the follies of youth behind me, I gazed up at the mountaintop. Got starry-eyed in the reflection of how we, the nethermost of creatures, might ascend to the empyreal heights. Where, I wistfully pondered, would such a rhapsodic journey begin? Then, a voice from afar, carried as though on the wings of the zephyr, whispered softly, "At the fount of H and H."

H and H?

Health and happiness.

The fountain of health and happiness on this planet?

Why else would the immortals deign to visit us! Ah, laddie, and there's the rub. The gods being what they are - avaricious, jealous, possessive - would pull out all stops to camouflage their great discovery.

The gods can be self-serving.

It became an Icarian undertaking. I tested thousands of solids, liquids, and gases. Hope would flame up only to be snuffed out in the crucible of despair. Promising leads led to cul-de-sacs. Weeks ran into months. The frustration spread into the marrow of my bones.

Yet you stuck with the game plan?

Slept little ... became irritable ... snapped at the plants and animals ... neglected the tomatoes ... ignored the birds ... Then one day I brushed up against an innocent-looking ever-green bush loaded with purple berries.

Purple berries?

Hardly worth a second glance. But when I took a step away, my S-S's buzzed like hummingbirds in heat.

You say purple berries?

Thought my time had run out.

Think I need a refill.

When the S-S's finally stopped vibrating, the "aha" bulb lit up. What could be a more ingenious camouflage than a plain,

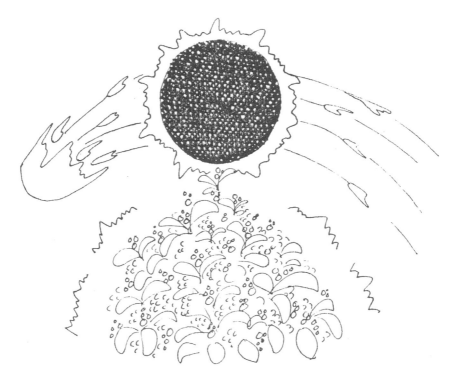

Eureka: The Juniper Bush

ordinary, garden-variety juniper? The road to nirvana had to pass through those berries.

What'd you do?

Resorted to trial and error. Boiled them, fried them, baked them, dried them, ate them raw. Nothing happened.

What was left?

I distilled them.

You what?

The sun went into an eclipse. A meteor lit up the sky. An event, m'lad, of astronomical proportions had taken place in the bowels of my woods.

Slightly about incredible!

But the 'fait' was not 'accompli'. The gods would, of course, demand exacting accoutrements.

(Hic) The gods can also be finicky.

I tried one combination after another.

Had to be an intoxicatin' experience!

Then, I recalled the mantra of the ascetics: the best things in life are simple. The Homeric search was over. The berry morphed into its final karma, the nectar of the gods, when it combined with six-parts geneva, a distilled rye grain, and one-part vitilis, a fermented albescent grape, accoutrements Anglo-Saxonized in the marketplace as gin and dry vermouth.

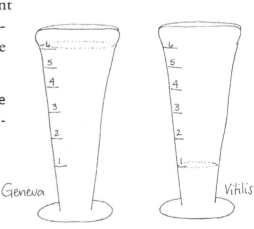

Geneva   Vitilis

Accoutrements

Holy mackerel, Grandfather, the very spirits with which we're celebratin' your birthday.

Not a thing wrong with your peepers, Grandson.

Am I hearin' right? You say you invented the martini?

(Sigh) I suffered the fate common to explorers of the universe. My ship pulled into dock too late. Was the nadir of my existence. The capstone of my labors, heralded by connoisseurs of the taproom as a monument of human triumph, is credited to a fly-by-night, flash-in-the-pan, illiterate Italian immigrant.

Somethin' tells me I haven't given the sauce its proper due. On the times that it's sent me tiptoein' through the tulips, I was totally ignorant of its health-restorin' properties. ... Wonder why the docs keep tellin' us that sauce in any form shortens life.

None are so blind as those who refuse to see. Look about you. How many more old sots do you see than old sawbones?

Grandfather, gettin' down to brass tacks, what's the nitty-gritty on this berry?

I recorded it in a scientific monograph: "The Miracle of Juniperus Communis". Never published it out of deference to your mother and the bootleggers.

Bootleggers?

Few display a more refined palate for the distilled product than those sensitive backwoods artisans. Notwithstanding, they've gone overboard for "white lightning", a liquescence of the corn grain. Despite the fabled claims, it can't hold a candle to the distillate of the berry. But I, for one, would be the last to puncture their bubble! The sight of glucose rising in the eyes of such gentle souls would simply take the iron out of the blood.

(Hic) Would make the strong cry. ... But back to the miracle.

In the treatise I chronicled the lip-to-liver odyssey of the peripatetic berry. That ordinary-looking, seed-bearing cone is a microbe tracer of the first water. As it weaves its way through the maze of capillaries, it spots and zaps all the freeloading cronies of the D-D's.

A back-up immunization system.

The versatile berry is also a throwback to old show biz. While zigging and zagging through the labyrinth of vessels, it puts on pantomime reminiscent of vaudeville's finest hour. The low comedy fractures the S-S's. Those warm camaraderie-feelings of bonhomie that characterize the civilized imbiber are simply his S-S's rolling in hysterics over the show.

Clear as a Swiss bell! The berry in distillation is changed into manna for our better angels. (Burp) What could be more edifyin' to the soul!

You've captured the quiddity, Grandson.

We better move on while the brain's still processin'. Because people are livin' longer, gerontology has become the hot science. The flood (hic) of research comin' out seems to agree that memory worsens with age.

Balderdash! Age has nothing to do with it.

Then why do old folks complain about pullin' blanks, forgettin' names, misplacin' items, whatever?

You're talking about fussbudgets who started life out that way.

But they say it gets worse with age.

More proof of what I'm saying.

Don't follow you.

Their memory's so rotten that they've forgotten how lousy it always was.

(Hic) Holds water. A flash! Bank on sieves, be all wet. … Grandfather, what would you say has bugged you the most in the golden years?

The body's center of gravity. The blooming idiot keeps rising. Changes life from growth and development to maintenance and repair.

A risin' center of gravity?

Nobody escapes it. It causes the top half of the body to shorten and our bottom half to lengthen.

What's so wrong with that?

Basic physics. A higher center weakens balance, making staying vertical more hazardous. When a spill occurs, recovery time is longer because the upper body has farther to fall. (Sigh) As the arms keep getting shorter and the legs longer, the day finally comes when only the acrobats of the world can put on their shoes and socks. … Growing old, m'lad, is not for sissies.

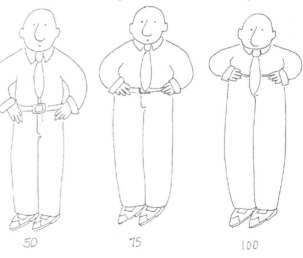

50   75   100

What Aging Does

If it's the body you say that changes most, why do we see so many seniles around?

They'd just done a better job of hiding it in their youth.

A flash! (Hic) Senility's a myth. All in the mind. ... Let's quickly jump into politics. Who's better at speakin' out of both sides of the mouth than politicians? And most of 'em are lawyers. What do you make of it?

No professionals, m'lad, treat the truth with more respect than the members of the bar. They respect it like a deadly poison. They handle it cautiously, use it sparingly, and keep it as far out of reach as possible.

How come?

A large sign hangs in law school: "Veritas stuns the intellect, shocks the emotions, shatters the will. Use only when con- ventional weapons fail."

How does justice ever prevail?

Through the balance principle.

Another gap in my education.

In the early years of prac- tice, the bungling coun- selor loses his innocent cases. They're found guilty. In the late years the moxie mouthpiece wins his guilty

Lawyer's Stock Room

cases. They're found innocent. Thus, in the end, all balances out.

What would make people ever want to take up the law?

Paranopathia limits the choices.

(Hic) No end to pathologies.

I described this one in Leslie's Weekly years ago. The magazine folded shortly afterwards.

What's it all about?

Old wine in a new bottle. A replay of the old melodrama of the irresistible force meeting the immovable object. The collision, however, takes place in inner space.

I'm still on square one.

The irresistible force is an insatiable craving for power, the immovable object a profound distrust of fellowmen. Courtesies such as friendly greetings are seen as tricks to take one off guard, chit-chats are taken as ploys for ulterior motives, innocent gestures taken as character digs, get-well cards as death wishes.

How can a power base be built without trustin' at least some people?

That's what brings on the lower back pains.

What got it started?

A serious flub of the pituitary.

Bad news. The master gland. What happened?

111

It activated the wrong color pigment in the urethra. Has everything coming out green.

No! Not what I think.

The color deepens over time. Barely noticeable in law school, the passed water takes on a chartreuse look after several years in court. By the time of an open judgeship, it's approaching a kelly green.

Never seen or heard the likes of it.

Nor ever will. It tops the list of life's unmentionables. Hypersensitivity, the core of the complex, intensifies the embarrassment. Attorneys mask their sensitive egos with a feigned happy-go-lucky air that diverts even their own prying, inquisitive mothers from ever suspecting the inner imperfection. Once the green becomes highly visible, the lads would risk a busted bladder to an unlocked water closet.

Do all lawyers (hic) have the imperfection?

Several inmates on death row made me the beneficiary of their wills to unravel the underlying dynamics of the prosecutor's cravings for the gas chamber. Observing their obsessive behavior for unlocked water closets had me using the money as bribes to loosen the tongues of our tight-lipped urologists. The amazing finding is that one American out of five will study law, and one American out of five will tint the commode green.

We've got that many lawyers?

Most of them keep it under hat. Once out of the hallowed halls, they'll front as bookies ... bill collectors ... glass blowers ... used-car salesmen ...

Why all the disguises?

> When the yellow's out of the urine, Grandson, one is disinclined to show his true colors.

All of this green reminds me of Uncle Sam. He keeps rollin' it off the presses. All because government got so big. What're your thoughts on it, Grandfather?

> The biggest kingfishes, beyond doubt, are those splashing about in the Potomac.

Yet our political science prof told us that democracy got into the business to spawn minnows.

> (Sigh) Accidents can occur even in the best regulated families.

In spite of it all - scandals, feathernestin', boondogglin', pork-barrelin' - the government has done some good things.

> I'm sure you're right. Would you care to share one?

What about the food stamp program?

> A good beginning.

It guarantees that nobody starves. What could be more humane?

> If you overlook the red tape, overhead, mismanagement, and rip-offs, it's government at its best.

(Burp) How could it be run differently?

> By trimming the waste and ensuring justice for all.

In a federal program?

Wouldn't require a wizard at the helm. Just stack food cartons containing the daily requirements for the smart cells - not a crumb for the Dum-Dums - in handy locations. Have them spoil-proof and light enough for even the old and the infirm to tote home. Could also throw in a bone for the family pooch.

Sure would reduce the fat. But what's to stop the rip-off? What's to keep the rich from gettin' away with a free lunch?

Their Dum-Dums. The junk that moves in the food markets makes it all too clear who makes up the shopping list.

A flash! The poor will inherit the earth. No pimples, heartburn, gas, whatever. Might see the big wheels in the drug empire flock to the bars to drown their sorrows.

Might see something even more novel - those with a natural antipathy toward work, the youth of our nation, deserting the beaches to check out the want ads.

Just the right tonic for the taxpayer. You should write the president. He needs all the help and advice he can get.

Too old for another invasion, Grandson.

Speakin' of desertin', the old gang's bustin' up - plungin' into the sea of matrimony. Water's great but the drownin' rate's out of sight! One buddy, down twice, has a rush order in to a bride-order house for an orphaned, deaf-and-dumb nympho who (hic) owns a liquor store. Why do you suppose so many marriages end up breakin' the vow till death do us part?

Poor mate selection. In the old days, nubile worth was judged by the size of the back: the bigger the better. Nowadays it's by

114

the size of the waist: the smaller the better. The hazard of a cute chick, m'lad, is that she has all the makings of henpecking.

Why do we keep on doin' it?

One invigorating spring day sashaying in the park taking in the seasonal insanity, my thoughts drifted to the electrodynamics of the gonads. How would they graph out? Would they show a pattern or would they show randomness? Time spent in the library was a washout. All the literature was on the plumbing. So I opened a new line of research. I discovered when sperms are charged, they generate two opposing currents, **agititus** and **cogititus**. Agititus plots out in short cycles and high spikes, cogititus, in long cycles and low spikes.

The devil did it to us again.

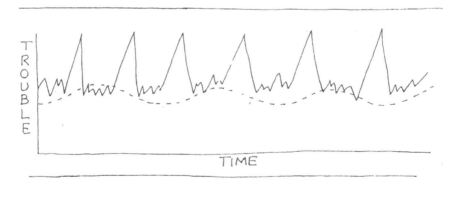

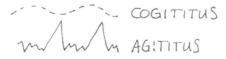

The Devil Did It to Us Again

High spikes trigger impulsivity: live for today ... full speed ahead ... make hay while the sun shines. Low spikes cotton to circumspection: look both ways ... check the guarantee ... read the fine print. Most of today's young bucks head for the sunny fields.

(Hic) Nothin' like those high spikes.

The currents are also very detectable in the use of language. Agititus slays the King's English - mixes metaphors, dangles participles, fragments sentences, turns strong nouns into weak verbs. But their strongest claim to fame is gilding the lily, coming up with such stunners as: God created the world so the two of us could meet. I'd climb Mount Everest for the next dance. The moon is a locket hanging on the chain of my love.

Oops!

Cogititus raises soul-searching questions like: When did you read your last book? Go to your last concert? Prepare a gourmet feast? How does your mother handle corn on the cob?

Now that's a difference that makes a difference.

Before hopping aboard the conjugal bandwagon, I suggest you check out her beverage cartons.

Why that?

I suspected a correlation between drinking habits and connubial bliss. Led me to inspect the homes of a group of distaffs addicted to the soda pops. The results turned out what I feared. Every one of them was a victim of early maternal deprivation, the worst prognosis for long-term relationships.

What was the evidence?

Walls lined with baby pics … closets jammed with shoes … medicine cabinets crammed with aspirins … (sigh) phone jacks in every room.

A flash! We are what we drink. (Hic) To save the holy institution of matrimony, we need to pass a constitutional amendment that bans the manufacture and sale of soft drinks. (Burp) By the way, Grandfather, what's so bad about a little gildin' of the lily?

Shattered illusions crack cups and a cracked cup is never the same.

Meanin'?

Meaning Cinderella grows faint on hearing that Prince Charming is phobic of heights. Her condition worsens on getting a second opinion on why the world was created. She had no desire to check on the composition of the moon.

Cracked cups make me think of cracked pots. And crackpots are on the rise. What's the answer?

A fascinating subject, **psychoceramics**. Had me doing a little snooping down at the loony bin.

Find out much?

The shrinks sidetracked me with buzzwords like genetic pre-disposition, childhood traumas, blood chemistry, hormonal imbalances, neurotransmitters - all about as useful for predict-ing lunacy as eye color for birth order.

More millions down the rat hole.

On tapping into their cortical circuits, I found what I long suspected.

What was that?

What makes them birds of a feather. All of them, regardless of color, creed, gender, or hat size, rated football the most exciting sport and baseball, the dullest.

No! Of the zillions of human variables and their zillions of combinations, the best predictor of insanity turns out to be the rank order of baseball and football! Now that's about a notch above human understandin'.

The takeover of the psyche, m'lad, is the supreme triumph of the Dum-Dums. But after a night of raucous celebration comes the dawn of sobering reality. They find that the brain's switchboard is too complex for their feeble mental powers. They keep punching the wrong keys.

So what do they do?

What anyone does when biting off more than one can chew - throw T-T's - temper tantrums. Shrinks keep missing what's right under their noses. The screaming meemies are nothing more than D-D's in T-T's.

Back to baseball and football. What makes them such powerful discriminators?

The challenges. The bigger they are the more they appeal to the S-S's. The smaller they are the more they appeal to the D-D's.

(Hic) Baseball's that much bigger a challenge than football?

Zounds, lad! In baseball, the object is to hit a five-ounce spheroid, three inches in diameter, traveling near 100 miles an hour. In football, the object is to hit a 300-pound meso-morph, a yard wide, traveling close to 10 miles an hour.

Point well taken. But, then, how do you account for all of the football fans still on the loose?

Commitment, in the final analysis, is a social issue. For the T-T's to qualify they have to be a public nuisance. Explains why the inmates in our institutions come from the city tenements, not the gated estates.

Somethin' to be said for the open frontier. … Is there any advanced warnin' of the tantrums?

The tip-off is a sudden drop in the quality of thought. The worst tailspin I've seen was that of All-American Amos "Fleetfoot" Finigan. He came to the cabin one day with that haunted look in his eye.

What was spookin' Fleetfoot?

He had sunk into a metaphysical quagmire, bogged down with such perplexities as: What kind of shoes does an angel wear to dance on the head of a pin? … If there are three persons in one god, why doesn't he see a psychiatrist? … If the eyes are the window of the soul, why aren't linebackers' black? … If God intended life to be more than making a touchdown, why did he shape the earth more like a football?

What'd you do?

I alerted his kinfolk where he was on the slippery slope and advised them to read up on the rights of visitors.

119

Grandfather, seems obvious to me we have to keep the D-D's from takin' over the psyche. How do we do it?

Find a good role model. … None better than the Babe.

Babe Ruth?

The sultan of swat was the epitome of dignified restraint. He never overburdened himself with the work ethic or overextended himself with exercise. Most he ever did was drift in the shade field and slowly circle the bases. He also avoided pseudo-intellectuals, never raising a question requiring more than a three-word answer. His mind at all times remained uncluttered.

Smart.

Brilliant! It staggers me to think of the number of S-S's that have to be coordinated to belt a blazing fastball the distance of his. He got my write-in vote for president during the depression.

The man with the big club presidential timber? (Hic)

Imagine what he would have done to the economy! America today would be rolling in 'diamonds'.

Somebody sure blew that one. … Grandfather, changin' subjects, there's somethin' I've been wantin' to ask you for a long time, but (hic) the time never seemed right.

Take another sip, m'lad. It does wonders for making times seem right.

It's been said that those who hear a different drummer begin life on a different beat. I'm thinkin', for example, of Halley's Comet

welcomin' in Mark Twain, and of Sigmund Freud's first squall comin' in the caul. What do you suppose the seismograph read 89
years ago?

Sipping also does wonders for the imagination. The day, according to all reports, was of little mark on land, sea, or sky.
However, it did rather charm your great-grandmother, a fan-
cier of the occult, to read of a new star sighted at the time of
my entry. When so informed, I warned that I'd sabotage any
plan to hitch my wagon to it.

A portent, Grandfather, not to be taken lightly. Know anything
more about it?

Slipped my mind until I ran into our local stargazer several
years ago. He checked the logs and found that the star be-
longed to a distant galaxy. I popped a suspender button on
catching the name.

What's it called?

Geneva. In honor of the Swiss observatory first sighting it.

Wooee, Grandfather! (Burp) It looks to me like your wagon was
hitched to a star after all. ... (Hic) Sure glad this is bein' recorded.
Only the good Lord knows what's goin' on in my storage cells.

Nothing to be alarmed about. The D.J.B.'s are simply per-
forming up to their usual standard. The burps and hics are
telling me that your Smart-Smarts have come out of their dol-
drums and are doing a number on your Dum-Dums.

Not hearin' a peep out of you. Guess who's overloaded with the little devils? ... We're windin' down to the final spins. Time left for only
a few quickies. I reached the conclusion one day, after reviewin'

the options, that the quickest way to fame and fortune is to write the great American novel. So, I took in a lecture on creative writin' to pick up pointers as to what turns out the Joyces, Hemingways, Faulkners, whoever. (Hic) Naturally, walked out empty-handed. If the genie were to grant me a wish, Grandfather, what should it be?

> The moxie when writing with tongue in cheek and cheek in tongue to keep folks guessing which is which.

What's the advantage in that?

> It's in the nature of the human beast to resolve ambiguity with prejudice and then credit the brilliance to the author. The ploy is a cinch to land a leg on a Pulitzer.

Pretty sneaky! Like in the ink-blot test, you see the sexy broads and admire the shrink's taste. Writin', then, boils down to bein' nothin' more than just a game.

> As is all of life, Grandson. But don't knock it. Games can be fun if played well, but not seriously. Never lose the sense of humor. We enter the casino of life flat broke so take each chip won as a bonus. Live to the fullest. Only a silly pack rat hoards his winnings because the chips have to be cashed in at the end. The Houdini is yet born who can convert them into traveler's checks.

I'm getting the message. It's better to live rich and die poor than to live poor and die rich.

> Attitude is of the essence. Pity the player insisting the world owes him a stake. Entitlement leads to disillusionment and that leads to cynicism. Life to a cynic is a shell game.

Never have liked shell games. Grandfather, if we were to make life a poker game, what would be your choice for a hole card?

> Fishing for a flight into fantasyland, eh! Why not! Too much reality makes Jack a dull boy. So, I rub the genie's lamp, make a wish, say abracadabra, and voilà, I've got what I've envied most of the gods, the magic of incarnation. I can be whatever I want, whenever I want, wherever I want. Today, I can be an eagle and soar above the clouds; tomorrow, a sea devil and roam the ocean floors; the day after, a gazelle and frolic in fields of clover. What exhilaration to escape the hidebound self, a self limited to one set of filters, to see only with human eyes, hear only with human ears, smell only with human nostrils! What a hoot to be able to cruise through life free of barriers to experience. … Holy jumping catfish!

The ultimate free spirit! (Hic) But hidebound as the devil's made us, what would you do differently were you to do it over again?

> Why, start sooner, of course, on the noble quest. The frittered away years not only delayed spiritual growth but deprived me of a place in the sun. Martini graces the menus of every bar and bistro in the land. … Where in tarnation do you see Leonardo!

The fickle twist of fate! One more quickie. What good word of advice for us grads?

> History warns us today's truths may be tomorrow's myths. The only certainty in life is change. Foolish consistency, as you know, is the hobgoblin of little minds. Thus, my message is simply this: either hone the adaptive skills to meet the challenges of change or get prepared to exit the way of the dinosaur.

(Hic) A Commencement Address rolled up into one sentence! ... I've good news to report. The blahs are finally gone. Gas is returnin' to the corpse, er, corpus. The fog has lifted. I say, let the green monster flash his trick mirror and try to sucker me into another wild-goose chase. Should he pull that trick, I'll unsheathe the sword and lop off his head. That's what I'll do: zip, zap, and decap!

Miracles never cease! ... I believe, m'lad, you've somehow overcome the odds and are over the hump. Even showing signs of a sense of humor and seeing the comical side of life. But now that the world is your oyster, be sure the pearl's not thrown out with the shell.

On returnin' you'll see the new marvel.

Don't put all your chips on it.

Whattaya mean, Grandfather?

Was over a fortnight ago. Not a candle was burning up yonder. The air was heavy. Nature still. I battened down the hatches. Then, the wind began rustling through the pines. A hound bayed. A thunderclap burst. I pulled up the blankets, snuggled in, and had a dream...

In livin' color? (Burp)

A phantasmagoria of my life: the fishing creek, the tomato patch, the house that Ruth built. Tramping in the rain, sloshing through snow, sniffing the wildflowers. As the poet would say, seeing an iris gleaming like a burnished dove. Then my all-time favorite goose waddled in, the one whose ass could soar the highest. She let out a cackle that echoed through the hollow, and then, she laid the biggest egg I ever did see. I picked it up, turned it over, and there it was, dead center.

What?

The numbers.

What numbers?

"Three" and "thirty".

That clairvoyant three again. What could it mean? (Burp) The time of day, Grandfather?

(Sigh) The time of night, Grandson - three score and thirty! (Hic)

POSTSCRIPT

It was my last night in Paris. I was sipping a martini at a sidewalk cafe on the Left Bank in Paris. It was a starry night. The soft murmur of the Seine was below me. A gusty wind had put a chill in the air. I was purposely alone. I raised my glass in a toast: to fewer narcs ... to more sluggers like the Babe ... to redder tomatoes ... to higher-flying asses ... to all the things dear to Grandfather. It was his 90th birthday.

My mind flashed back to his caveat before I went overseas. He told me not to be hoodwinked by a theory whose popularity rests on its flattery to the vanity. To show its lack of substance, play the devil's advocate, propose a contrary theory which, too, lacks validating data and differs only in that it's unflattering to the vanity. See how far you get with it. I have found the ploy invaluable, he added, particularly when the conversation gets more emotional than enlightening. I have savored the advice through the years.

I chanced to glance up and saw a star streaking through the sky. The winds stilled. The Seine hushed. The chill deepened in my bones. I knew in my heart that the circle had closed. Grandfather was gone. It must have been a helluva fight. A star rose on the day of his coming and a star fell on the day of his leaving. How about that! Holy jumpin' catfish!

Then, a pervasive calm descended over me. I nodded to the garcon and ordered a refill. ... Grandfather would have wanted it just that way.

A Final Toast